Microscopic Me

Unless otherwise indicated, all scripture quotations are taken from the *King James Version* of the Bible.

Scripture quotations marked (NIV) are taken from the *Holy Bible, New International Version*®, NIV®.
Copyright © 1973, 1978, 1984 by Biblica, Inc.™
Used by permission of Zondervan. All rights reserved worldwide.

Microscopic Me

Microscopic Me

Tiffany L. Bride

Table of Contents

Introduction

He's guaranteed the end; you know the beginning. All that stands between the two is a life altering choice. A heavenly host anxiously awaits the moment for standing ovation. Clenched to the edge of their seats, they watch a plot of triumph and victory, overcome and defeat, love and devotion unfold in the moving saga of your life. The script was written by line to be executed with precession and commitment. No understudy can play the role only one was destined to perform. It headlines your name. The light of life shines upon you and puts you in best view for the entire world to see His glory.

The choice is simple and outcome certain. Success, elation, and abundance beyond measure come with performing as the Almighty directs. Knowing the outcome of tomorrow minimizes the mishaps of today. The lines stumbled over in dress rehearsal help to perfect the ultimate delivery. Those lines aren't repeated, but used to elevate skill. One can only give the truest performance and receive destined glory by having a solid sense of self. Who is the person beneath the makeup and costume, behind the backdrop, props, and surroundings? Is confidence in delivery exhibited or is every line being fed from the pit below? A microscopic view reveals all, and allows the restoration of even the tiniest blemish and smallest fray. Understanding your role, as well as the riches, wealth, and influence attached, first starts with peeling back the layers to see the microscopic me.

chapter 1

<u>Act One, Scene One</u>

ACT ONE, SCENE one. The curtain rises with you at center stage. You stand there accompanied by a plethora of individuals, some who will play a major role in your life and others who will only state a few lines, and soon be forgotten. But as the main character in the story of your life, the entire production moves and revolves around your words, actions, feelings, thoughts, and beliefs. No matter how elaborate the wardrobe or eloquent the speech, the success or failure of the performance is contingent upon who you allow to direct your life.

The introductory scene is important. It establishes a plot; it alludes to a theme, and it hints to an outcome. Though you have lived your life from the beginning, it's imperative to understand how your story ties into the backdrop created long before you ever graced the stage. That is where we'll start, act one, scene one, Genesis, the beginning.

Genesis means beginning. It's the first scene of an epic journey. In the beginning God created all that there is. Look around you. Look to your left and to your right. Now take a glance over your shoulder. All that you see, God created. It may be hard to image how God created your house when you watched the builders fulfill the blueprint design. Or you may grapple with the idea that your dream car that takes you from point A to point B every day did not generate from some assembly line. The label on your shirt may read "Made in Taiwan", but I assure you that every thread, piece of machinery, and person used to make that warm, cozy blouse that you love to wear so much on Tuesday and every other Sunday, came from the earth. In the beginning, before there were any designer labels or boutique stores, God created the heavens and the earth.

There wasn't form to the earth when God began creating. There was nothing but a blank canvas to paint. So God, being the artisan that He is, began to work on His masterpiece, one intended to last eternally. His words were the paint and His voice was the brush used to create His great work.

Unlike the on demand, instantaneous, I want it now world we live in, the earth's creation wasn't as such. God took time to craft them. He handmade every man, woman, and child, added his designer details and intricacies that were so fine and meticulous that even under a microscope there was no fray in appearance. There couldn't be because it was made by Him. Certainly God in His almighty nature could have roared from above and spoke the world into existence in one breathe. However, He shows us from the very beginning of time His character. He exemplifies how patient He is and how He commands the best.

We see in Genesis, at the end of each day of creation, God evaluated what He had made and noted that it was "good." His design was not average, subpar, or doable. He created top quality. This is because God's standards supersede any standard or level of expectation that man could have. Because God's standards are so high, when God said His creations were "good," what He made was the absolute best, no less than who He is.

Picture the earth as our home. Anyone who has ever purchased or rented a home knows that there is a time of preparation before the inhabitants can move in. The walls may call for bright fuchsia paint to contrast the apple green couch. Furniture has to be arranged perfectly to allow the free flow of movement. Accents, throws, and decorative items are strategically placed to create that placid, at home feeling. The desired environment may be different for everyone, but the results are the same. When all has been designed and put into place, the inhabitants are ready to move in.

When God made our current dwelling place, He made it so that all of its inhabitants would have that "at home" feeling. We would have a high level of comfort and security in our own skin. The beautiful, soft, well-formed vessels He created to house the spirits of His daughters were made softer and more comfortable than cashmere. All would share feelings of security, comfort, fulfillment, and relaxation. And in our state of comfort, we would lounge in the leaves, enjoy the cool of the day, and let spring water flow gently over our feet. Everything truly was good, made by God for us to enjoy and to serve Him with.

To serve in the way God intended was not associated with thoughts of hard labor, requiring an absorbent amount of energy, or undesirable works of the hand. We were formed with the intent to fellowship with God, to talk to Him, spend time with Him, and take care of the earth He gave us. We were to serve Him with our company, worship Him with our talents, and love Him with all of our hearts as Deuteronomy 6:5 tells us to.

"5And thou shalt love the LORD thy God with all thine heart, and with all thy soul, and with all thy might."

It was man's disobedience to God in this first scene that cut us short of the fullness of life He created us for.

Has there ever been a time that you just wanted to kick yourself because you missed out on a great opportunity? You didn't listen to sound advice; you were impatient, possibly even stubborn. God gave clear instructions and you decided to take a detour. That is what happened to man in the beginning. The disregard of the Lord's instructions removed the roadblock to sin and put us on a bumpier, less pleasurable path than the one He already paved. However, God sent us His son Jesus to steer us back to Him. Jesus took on human form and served as an example by living a blemish free life. Then He submitted to a brutal death, one of torture, ridicule, and chastisement, so that we could all be saved through faith and return to our Father who created us. This is evident in John 1:10-14. It is through faith that we are able to tap into our inheritance, one of eternal life and fulfilled living. Though the enemy comes to take away all you have, to kill you hopes and dreams, and to ultimately destroy your entire life, Jesus came so that we could not just have life, but have life in abundance.

> "*10The thief cometh not, but for to steal, and to kill, and to destroy: I am come that they might have life, and that they might have it more abundantly.*"
> John 10:10

Every person has a beginning, a genesis, a place where they were born, raised, taught and molded. We all have roots grounded in a particular lifestyle. Some come from a single parent home; others may have lived with an extended family. There are those who were born into families of wealth, while others worked three jobs to barely pay the bills. Some bear fruit from the pain endured as a victim of violence or substance abuse. There are those who hold feelings of neglect stemming from working parents that never seemed to have time to show them love as Christ does His children. Irrespective of background, each person has a beginning, a genesis, a place where roots were established.

At times it may appear that some are more fortunate than others because they had a better beginning. We know from Acts 10:34 that God is not a respecter of persons; He doesn't play favorites. He loves us all the same. He will not do for one what He is not willing to do for all.

"34Then Peter began to speak: "I now realize how true it is that God does not show favoritism" NIV

So what is it that makes the positive difference in how we live and experience life? It's taking directions from Jesus. Yes, it's that simple. Once you make the decision to give your life back to the one who made it, you are immediately planted into the kingdom of heaven. Your roots are embedded in fertile ground and they have no choice but to yield mouthwatering fruit. Jesus said in John 8:12,

"12Then spake Jesus again unto them, saying, I am the light of the world: he that followeth me shall not walk in darkness, but shall have the light of life."

Because you have Jesus in your life, you have all the light you need for growth and productivity.

Imagine the little plant on your desk at work. The leaves are sagging and becoming wilted. There are no windows to provide sunlight and the variable office temperature does not provide a suitable environment for growth. Though the plant is watered from time to time, it isn't long before the leaves start to whiter again. As children of God, we are the same. We need to be watered daily with His word to experience the light of His promise, which guides our walk with him. Being in the right spiritual environment also allows us to be nourished, to grow, and to be whole as God intended.

Once you are in Christ, your life has an entirely new beginning, a grander stage, and a new backdrop for your life. Second Corinthians 5:17 says,

> "*17Therefore if any man be in Christ, he is a new creature: old things are passed away; behold, all things are become new.*"

Many times people live relishing on prior scenes, past hurts or former fears. "If only I could change this, or if only that didn't happen," some say. Well, we can't change it, and it did happen. No matter how disappointing, embarrassing, or painful the situation was, we don't have the capacity to erase the series of events; but Jesus does. He comes and washes every bad thing away and gives us a fresh start. How awesome is that?

Think about when you sign up for a gym membership. You have something that you wish to accomplish. You want to slim the waist or build your quadriceps. In order to have access to the equipment, you have to sign a contract, put down a deposit, and pay a monthly fee. Most classes are included in the membership, but they are only available at certain times and have limited capacity. During high peek hours there are periods of waiting. All of the treadmills are full and two elliptical machines are out of order. With God, you receive a lifetime membership with unlimited benefits, free of charge. There are no loopholes or deceiving contract terminology. You have unlimited access. Whatever you wish to accomplish in Him, He will work out. God always answers, and always delivers according to His word. If your name hasn't already been signed into the book of life, there is only one action required to become a member.

> "⁹*That if thou shalt confess with thy mouth the Lord Jesus, and shalt believe in thine heart that God hath raised him from the dead, thou shalt be saved.*"
> Romans 10:9

If you confessed it and truly believe it, then welcome to your new beginning, **act one, scene one**.

chapter 2

The BIG Question

ONCE YOU'VE had the phenomenal experience of making Christ the director of your life and having Him give you a new start, the transformation process continues. For as many years as you have been alive, your sense of self and identity were likely sculpted by the world's perspective and not God's. Your purpose is all found in Him, who you are, and who you are to become has divine destiny attached to it.

Identity. Where did I come from? Where am I going? Does anyone have a roadmap into destiny? Identity is something that many people struggle with. Some struggle for a short period of time, others their entire lives. We go to sleep and wake up each morning in the same skin we went to bed in the night before. We see our faces in the mirror, know our bodies, and understand our general likes and dislikes. With the exception of the effects of time, we look the same, sound the same, and smell the same. But who are we really? A person without purpose is aimlessly wandering in life. The activities of work, home, and school are all rote. What gives purpose and life to the state of being alive is Christ. The questions of who am I and why am I here are answered in Him. Certainly if you seek Him, you will discover the answers you seek.

Lack of knowing one's identity can create a void. The sense of security desired turns into insecurity. All that we do is questioned and who we are to become is pondered repetitively. A common saying is, *If you don't know where you are, how do you know where you are going?*" The incessant condition of being lost creates a need for direction. "*Going somewhere is better than going nowhere.*" This mentality is a trap, a pool of quicksand that slowly sucks you in and swallows you whole. Drug addiction, alcoholism, promiscuity, and abusive relationships, are often used as fillers for the lack of sense of self. For someone else the filler may be constant work, keeping preoccupied with activities, severe depression, or anxiety. The world has many vices to fill the void as well as astute distractions from your real purpose. Like opposite poles of a magnet, we are drawn to our creator. It is the world's job and the functionality of sin to distort your spiritual connection and draw us into a life that is too busy and distant from Christ.

Every woman was created for a purpose. Each of us has worth and is highly valued of the Lord. Thus the journey of searching and philosophical pondering can end. We were created by God to love Him, to worship Him, to do a great work, and to live a fulfilled life. The skills and talents you have, God gave them to you. If He hasn't already, He will reveal your destiny. We, as women, are extremely important in the kingdom. Understanding that you were made for greatness is the first step to crushing any feelings of inadequacy and doubt of self-worth.

If someone was asked to describe the characteristics of a woman, a typical response may be that women are intuitive, witty, sensible, compassionate, dedicated, nurturing individuals. Women are the glue that holds the family intact, the mood setters and dream motivators. We have a mind like a steel trap, having a divine capacity to remember. Whenever something is missing, we are the ones our families come to.

"Honey have you seen my keys," a husband asks?

"On the kitchen counter," we respond.

"Mom, where is my soccer uniform," the kids pose a half an hour before the game?

"Hanging in the wash room," we reply with such patience, most of the time.

From our diligent hands homes are beautifully decorated, delicious meals prepared, living environments kept clean and comfortable. The organizational support of new business ventures, loud applause after a dance recital, or excited utterance of "Good job" for A's and B's on a report card all flow from the hearts and mouths of women. It is not coincidental or of societal design that women are able to multitask, think quickly on their feet, or support their families. Women are inherently designed by God to be that way.

The amazing characteristics women possess stem from creation. After God created man, He took inventory of all of His creation. He observed the birds in the vast sky, fish swimming in the sea, and every other animal that walked the earth. Subsequent to His evaluation, God realized,

> "[18]*And the LORD God said, It is not good that the man should be alone; I will make him an help meet for him.* [21]*And the LORD God caused a deep sleep to fall upon Adam, and he slept: and he took one of his ribs, and closed up the flesh instead thereof;* [22]*And the rib, which the LORD God had taken from man, made he a woman, and brought her unto the man.* [23]*And Adam said, This is now bone of my bones, and flesh of my flesh: she shall be called Woman, because she was taken out of Man.*"
> Genesis 2:18, 21-23

We see from the genesis of creation, women were made to be a suitable helper for man. *"Is that all I am here for, to* serve *a man?"* No, that is not your sole purpose but it is one of them. We were not created to serve in a negative sense, but to help. There is a clear distinction. To help means to assist, counsel, support, facilitate, and strengthen. To serve in a negative connotation means to work for or to be in bondage to. Jesus, our savior, even understood the importance of serving. He himself modeled how men are to serve each other. Prior to the Passover Feast, Jesus washed the feet of His disciples. The ultimate sacrifice of love would be made through the relinquishment of His life; but He demonstrated acts of love and service on every level, both grand and small.

> "[14] *If I then, your Lord and Master, have washed your feet; ye also ought to wash one another's feet.* [15] *For I have given you an example, that ye should do as I have done to you.* [16] *Verily, verily, I say unto you, The servant is not greater than his lord; neither he that is sent greater than he that sent him.* [17] *If ye know these things, happy are ye if ye do them.*"
> John 13:14-17

Service is an expression of love. It doesn't matter who you are, what family you belong to, or how much money you have. Your position and status are balanced weights on a heavenly scale. The son of God, our savior, washed the feet of twelve men. Those feet walked dusty roads and were probably callused from traveling bumpy paths. The Lord used His clean hands to soothe worn soles. Women are to serve and to soothe just like Christ.

Performing acts of service seems to collide at times with the ideology of the "independent woman." Nothing is wrong with a woman that works hard, has a career, and can use her God given talents. Who or what is it that some women are seeking to be independent from? Is it from a man? Is it from falling into the traditional roles? Or is it that some are inadvertently seeking independence from God? We were formed from a piece taken from man, thus we have the ability and DNA to function as man. What we were created from is not what we were created for. A coup of household headship removes man from His assigned seat and you from yours. That is why when attendance is taken, we find a lot of men marked absent because they are not in their assigned seat. By withholding yourself from marriage, a particular occupation, or other role assigned to women, you may be running from what God has specifically purposed for your life. The truth is that we were not created to be alone. God made us to be in relationship with Him first and man second. *I'm never going to get married,* some will say. That is possible, but allow the direction to come from God. You may discover new, exciting attributes about yourself and fulfill a plan for the Lord within your marriage.

Once you have received direction from the Lord on His marital plans for your life and accepted your role as helper, there are some fundamental elements to understand. You were designed to be suitable for a particular person, a match, a pair, a fit. A Heart and a Club are not like suites. Like oil and water, they don't go together. They actually repel each other. Have you ever wondered why you and the person you are dating seem to recoil from each other? You try again and again to gel but it just doesn't work. That's because God has a person for you that is your exact match. Women were formed from the rib of a man. That means that we are a missing part of them. They need us to do what a rib is suppose to do, help support the chest cavity and protect the vital organs. Without a suitable helper, man is missing part of his structure, a piece of his support. Vital parts of his life need you to completely fulfill their function. You have to understand that you are greatly needed.

Imagine how vulnerable the heart would be without a rib cage to protect it. It would be more susceptible to attack, easily wounded. It could loose its rhythm if thumbed the wrong way. Even the absence of one rib could produce a small entry point to disaster. Doesn't it amaze you that God could have chosen any part of the body to mold a woman from, but He chose a piece that had great importance, a piece that helps to protect the man's most vital organ.

What happens if a man's heart stops beating? Blood stops flowing to the brain, and he can no longer think. And if his brain can't send a signal to his lungs, the man can no longer breathe. With the secession of a beating heart and inhalation of breathe, comes loss of life. Why would God pull us from such an important piece of a man and not perhaps from fatty tissues, from a bone between his toes, or from muscles on his back? It is because women are important and are greatly needed. We aren't excess, like fat that can be burned while running on a treadmill. We are the head and certainly not beneath the feet of others. Nor are we a second thought, completely ignored unless one turns around. No, we are a rib. We support as Christ created us to. We help to keep man in rhythm with God's word by being obedient ourselves. We understand the importance of keeping the heart pumping, brain moving, and oxygen flowing so that the man can live the life called by God.

Like a present received for a special occasion, when God presented woman to man, God knew that she would be pleasing to him. She would invoke emotions of joy and happiness. She would be an expression of Christ's love for him. This is another point to note, we are pleasing. God only presents His best. Man was so pleased with what God blessed him with that he took immediate ownership for woman. Though she is an individual, she is a part of man. The two are connected. Imagine two round gears whose teeth interlock, as one gear turns so does the other. If one gear stops moving the other can keep it going by its continual movement. Neither gear can ever stop churning so long as the other is moving. First Peter 3:1-2 says,

> "*¹Wives, in the same way be submissive to your husbands so that, if any of them do not believe the word, they may be won over without words by the behavior of their wives, ²when they see the purity and reverence of your lives.*" NIV

As a partner and helper, a woman serves as one of the greased gears that keep the relationship moving along the path of God.

The act doesn't conclude and story end after a woman marries. The newly united couple move into the next scene. They begin to build what is in God's blueprint for them. God tells His people in Jeremiah 29: 4-6 to increase. They are to construct homes and settle down. They must plant to live off of the harvest. There is to be a constant state of progression, increasing and not decreasing.

Another part of our identity is being settled. God desires for us to become settled, not just in the sense of geographic location but also in the sense of establishing a strong relationship grounded in Him. If the two are contending, not operating as one, still trying to figure things out, they are not ready to produce what God is trying to grow from the two. You can't eat unless there is a harvest. You can't harvest unless you sew. And you can't sew if you have no place to plant. It is important to be settled within your self as well as settled were the Lord leads. Sew how He tells you, and eat the fruit He provides.

When you find yourself in His settled place, production occurs. Children can grow because you are grounded in God and you have the ability to nurture them in the ways of the Lord. Resources are also rooted in a settled atmosphere. The Bible says that gardens will be planted and bring forth. This means that when you are where God has called you to be, your businesses and other works of the hand will be productive. You experience increase and forward progression when in the place God directs.

In addition to being helpers, builders and producers, we also have skills assigned by God to help fulfill our purpose. Romans 12:6-8 says,

> "⁶We have different gifts, according to the grace given us. If a man's gift is prophesying, let him use it in proportion

to his[a] faith. [7]If it is serving, let him serve; if it is teaching, let him teach; [8]if it is encouraging, let him encourage; if it is contributing to the needs of others, let him give generously; if it is leadership, let him govern diligently; if it is showing mercy, let him do it cheerfully." NIV

Whatever our spiritual gifts are, we are to use them to the glory of God. They are not present for idle use or to be a topic of icebreaking conversation. Your gift has a way of being just that, a gift. You already possess it. It won't cost a thing to share it with someone else. The neat part about it is that you will always have more to share the more you give. You never know how much of a blessing you can be in someone's life, while blessing yours all the same.

What happens when God tells us to do something for Him and we don't have the talent needed to complete the process? You have the eggs but no flour. You have vanilla but no milk. How can you make the cake without all of the ingredients? Everything else is already on the stove, so you can't leave the house. What do you do? You call your husband, tell him what you need to finish and wait until he comes back from the store with the rest of the ingredients. We do the same with God. We have talents but need God to fill the places where we lack the ingredients. When God calls you to do something that can't be performed with your current level of ability, He bridges the gap. He brings you whatever is missing so that you can finish the work. That is why He is God. He has everything we need.

In Exodus, God wanted Moses to build. To complete God's assignment for that moment skills, tools and resources were required.

> *" ¹ Then the LORD said to Moses, ² "See, I have chosen Bezalel son of Uri, the son of Hur, of the tribe of Judah, ³ and I have filled him with the Spirit of God, with skill, ability and knowledge in all kinds of crafts- ⁴ to make artistic designs for work in gold, silver and bronze, ⁵ to cut and set stones, to work in wood, and to engage in all kinds of craftsmanship. ⁶ Moreover, I have appointed Oholiab son of Ahisamach, of the tribe of Dan, to help him. Also I have given skill to all the craftsmen to make everything I have commanded you:"*
> Exodus 31:1 -6 NIV

As exemplified in the word, God always provides the resources needed. If He doesn't give us the skill directly, He will put someone in our lives to help us finish the work. Have you ever felt that another person was God sent? They were in the right place at the right time to help you out. *"That wasn't just coincidence?"* Not at all, they were a part of God's master plan. Wives are part of God's master plan for their husbands. That is why we are viewed as a jack of all trades. We were given many skills to help them with their tasks.

During the course of living, the Lord will place people in your life to help with your mission. Those individuals may be strangers, but they may also be friends and family. Often God puts us in relationship with people so that we can help each other on His assignments. It is vital to be mindful that there are people designed to assist; it is also important to have a watchful eye and attune ear those who seek to distract. Sometimes people are only to be present for a season. Like trees that shed their leaves in the fall, so are those who are not to move forward into our next season.

Jeremiah 29:8 -9 warns not to be deceived by lies because they do not come from God. If God has given an assignment, no man can alter it. Sometimes people will try to hinder your progression because of personal insecurity or jealously. Despite their motive, you must continue to press forward and ignore distractions. To distract means to take away attention or to pull out. Words and actions of another can be used to pull you out of the will of God. Sometimes the process of distraction is slow, like catching a fish. The bait rests in the water placidly and waits for you to approach. Once it has caught your eye, the distraction begins to reel in the bait slowly so that you follow. And as soon as you bite, it's caught you and yanks you right out of the living water. Why is the bait so appealing? It's because some distractions present themselves as if they were sent from God. But it's easy to know false advertisement when you see it. How? Because what the bait says contradicts what the word of God says. When distractions come into your life, even if visually appealing, don't blink an eye. God has something greater in your plan. No temporary appeasement, pit stop, or short-cut is worth jeopardizing the work you are investing in His will.

The microwave society we live in today encourages instant gratification. *"It would take less time to do it my way rather than God's way."* Ecclesiastes 9:11 says,

> *"[11] I have seen something else under the sun: The race is not to the swift or the battle to the strong, nor does food come to the wise or wealth to the brilliant or favor to the learned; but time and chance happen to them all."* NIV

Why rush, fight, pay, or reason to finish quicker if you are not going to achieve what God has destined for you. You may receive something, but something isn't the same as God's best thing. Follow His steps and stay the course. *"Well it didn't take so and so that long to get her..."* and then you go down the laundry list of things so and so possesses or has accomplished. You may not be aware of what that person went through to get where they are. They may not actually be where they are supposed to be and what they have now is only temporary. Or it may have been part of God's design that they reach their destination at that particular time. We shouldn't compare our purpose and plan to someone else's. That is why it is someone else's plan. It doesn't belong to you.

There is a popular saying, "looks can be deceiving." But according to the Word,

> *"[9] But as it is written, Eye hath not seen, nor ear heard, neither have entered into the heart of man, the things which God hath prepared for them that love him."*
> 1 Corinthians 2:9

chapter 3

Mirror, Mirror

THOUGH WE HAVE promises from God and great purpose attached to our lives, we don't always believe them. We look into the mirror and the reflection doesn't resemble what God says about us.

When was the last time you took a good look in the mirror? Is it when you were dressing for work, applying makeup as you backed out of the driveway, or trying on a dress in a department store? If that was the last time you took a good look at yourself, look again. Take a long, hard gaze. Turn to the side, profile a bit. Now, what do you see? Your answer should be, "The image of God here on earth." So many times our eyes deceive us. We look in the mirror and do not see a beautiful design. All we see is the extra weight we could loose, the bare, pale face that desperately needs makeup or we see nothing at all. We are so disgusted with ourselves that we rush past every mirror and don't bother to look up. However, it is important to look up to see what God sees and says about you, your image, and beauty.

When God decided to make us, He not only made man but He also made him an awesome sidekick, woman. Men and women alike are all children of God but each sex has unique features and composition. In Genesis 1:26, God made man in His image, and He gave man authority over the sky, sea, and every thing in-between.

"*26 Then God said, "Let us make man in our image, in our likeness, and let them rule over the fish of the sea and the birds of the air, over the livestock, over all the earth, [a] and over all the creatures that move along the ground." NIV*

Because we were made in His image, we were made to be a reflection of Him in the earth. There are instances though, when the reflection we see is distorted. It is like going to a carnival funhouse and standing in front of one of those "funny" mirrors that make us look short or fat, super skinny or way too tall. We know in our minds that despite what the mirror shows us, we don't appear that way in reality. The same is true with our Godly image. When we look in the mirror, we don't look the way our worldly eyes suggest, which is less than Jesus' 20/20. We often see ourselves as the media portrays.

So many magazines define fashion do's and don'ts. They tailor acceptable designs and colors that change with the seasons. With all the changes, it's hard to keep up. Yet, the magazines don't stop with style and dress.

They provide tips on ways to exercise so you can fit into a size two. Newsflash, not everyone was meant to be a size two; and everyone doesn't look good in lime green or whatever the color of the season may be. God wants His daughters to take care of their bodies, be healthy, and look good.

> "[19]Do *you not know that your body is a temple of the Holy Spirit, who is in you, whom you have received from God? You are not your own;*"
> 1 Corinthians 6:19 NIV

The Lord's house should not look a hot mess; we have to take care of ourselves. When we walk out the front door, we represent the body of Christ. There is beautiful clothing for every size and shape. Finding clothing that fits comfortably and colors that flatter, practicing good hygiene and living a healthy lifestyle is important in representing the body.

Every disease is under the authority of God. God has given us authority as well. We are to avoid lifestyles that can lead to acquiring ailments that will hinder our physical wellbeing as well as monitor blood presser and cholesterol levels. It's fine to enjoy snacks, but do so proportionately and provide the balanced diet your body needs.

Contrary to popular belief, what we look like really does matter, certainly not on a superficial level, but on a spiritual level. It's hard to keep the attention of someone you are trying to witness to if they are distracted by a wayward appearance. God is the best and needs us to represent Him by looking our best. Keep mints in your pocketbook, have a safety pin ready if something should snap. The little things matter because you never know when you will be needed to make a difference on a large scale. Looking good doesn't mean conforming to what the world's definition of beauty. God created us to be individuals, to have our own unique personalities and styles.

When we try to conform to what the world says we should look like, talk like, and act like, we put ourselves in a box. We stunt the process of growing into the women He fashioned. Sometimes we even fall into sin trying to obtain an image that was never our own. Envy and covetousness are not of God. When we begin to envy the gorgeous movie star or model, we are operating in sin. You'd probably be amazed at what the actress really looks like without the makeup, clothing, special lighting, and touchups. As the layers are peeled away, she looks less like a super star and more like an ordinary person. That is because she is just an ordinary person, whose occupation puts her on a public stage. She eats, she sleeps, and she works just like you. Who really makes a person look and feel their best is Jesus Christ.

If you want to be a super star, go to the author and finisher of faith. He will put His super on your natural, and there is no role you won't be cast as lead. The Bible tells us in Exodus 20:30 that we must not worship or believe in any other gods. Worshiping and idolizing a public image or any other person is a form of idolatry. We are to emulate God only and aspire to be more like Him everyday.

Another area where we can get ourselves into trouble is when we want what belongs to someone else. Often unmet desires transform into covetousness. We want nicer clothing, a larger home, a more luxurious car. We wish for longer hair, smoother skin, or some other change to our physical appearance. Exodus 20:17 instructs not to desire what someone else has. Why salivate over another's plate when you can have your own. That's silly. If you are at a five star restaurant and money is no object, you can order anything from the menu. You don't have to order an appetizer as an entree. The Lord will give you what you desire, so long as you follow Him.

For example, you can't ask God for your sister's husband. He belongs to your sister. God can and will bless you with the husband He specifically created for you. No matter how mean your boss is, you can't pray that he choke to death and expect God to answer that prayer. God stands by His word and He can't contradict what He has already said. Thus, He will not commit a sinful act or something detrimental to you or others because you think it will make you feel better for the moment. What you ask for has to align with what is in His word. That is why we pray as Matthew 6:10 says and to pray,

"*10Thy kingdom come, Thy will be done in earth, as it is in heaven.*"

Have you ever reached a point when God granted every petition but you still remained unsatisfied; you remained in a continual state of feeling unworthy or inadequate? When this happens, you may be suffering from something I like to call the "Enough Syndrome." *"I am not pretty enough." "I am not skinny enough." "I am not wealthy enough." "I am not smart enough."* On and on the thoughts go and never stop. In your convoluted eyes, you are never enough. Enough for whom? God made us. We are certainly enough in His eyes. Matthew 10:30-31 tell us that God values us greatly. So much that He knows how many hairs are on our heads, meaning He knows our intricacies. Things you don't even know about yourself, He does. You are so valuable that He paid the price of sin and death with the sacrifice of His only son.

The reason why we don't feel like we are enough is because we are placing our value in things and people. *"I am somebody if I am CEO of a company." "I am important so long as my boyfriend never leaves me." "As long as I have platinum credit status, I am really worth something."* Those worldly things are immaterial. You could get laid off of your job, your significant other could break up with you tomorrow, and because you lost your job, you loose your home, car, and platinum credit status. If you find your identity in anything other than God, you will loose yourself when those things falter. One may fall into deep depression, experience anxiety, suffer from anorexia, bulimia, or other types of disorders, all because of a distorted view of value. It is true that God gives us access to His riches and glory while we are here on earth, but our self-worth does not rest in possessions or relationships other than the one with Him.

Changing your perspective by renewing your mind helps to overcome disillusionment. Romans 12: 1—3 states,

> "¹*I beseech you therefore, brethren, by the mercies of God, that ye present your bodies a living sacrifice, holy, acceptable unto God, which is your reasonable service. ²And be not conformed to this world: but be ye transformed by the renewing of your mind, that ye may prove what is that good, and acceptable, and perfect, will of God. ³For I say, through the grace given unto me, to every man that is among you, not to think of himself more highly than he ought to think; but to think soberly, according as God hath dealt to every man the measure of faith.*"

Your body and image are a reflection of the Lord, it is holy and pleasing to Him, and its uses are an act of worship. What does your worship consist of? Are you running to the bathroom after every meal, shoving your finger down your throat? Is your frame weak and frail because you refuse to nourish your body? Do you wear long sleeves in ninety-eight degree weather to hide the self inflicted cuts and bruises? Does your worship to God entail hating yourself so much that you allow others to abuse you physically or emotionally?

We are to praise God with our bodies, how we live and carry ourselves. We are esteemed through Him not through a television program, book, or individual.

Though we live in the world, we are not part of it. Psalms 8:4-5 says,

> "⁴*What is man, that thou art mindful of him? and the son of man, that thou visitest him? ⁵For thou hast made him a little lower than the angels, and hast crowned him with glory and honour.*"

God thinks of us and visits us. He made us to be rulers. Are we not daughters of the Almighty God, the king of everything? As members of the royal family, we were given authority over the earth. Finding your true identity involves renewing your mind.

Along with changing thinking patterns, it is important to pray and take action. Earlier, in Genesis 1:26 we noticed that God gave us dominion over the earth. Therefore some things we don't have to ask God for, they are already under our authority. If you want to change your hair color or length, go to salon and get your hair done. If you need a new look, go purchase clothing from a store that sells apparel within your budget. If you want to loose some weight, exercise and change eating habits. No need to fret over the solution to a problem that is already answered. If you need help or guidance in these areas, God will certainly assist you. Any other desire that you may have, such as finding a husband, obtaining a home or transportation, pray to God and believe Him for your desire. Absolutely nothing is outside of His authority.

Lastly, we must spend time with God, reading the word and worshiping daily. The inner beauty caused by the presence of the Holy Spirit will radiate to the outside world. People will notice that there is something different about you.

"Have you changed your hair," they will ask.

"No," you respond.

"That must be a new outfit?"

"I've had this for years."

"Then you must have lost some weight."

"Thank you, but no."

People without Christ in their life won't be able to put their finger on it, but they will see you in a new light, the light of life. Use their inquiry as a perfect opportunity to witness. Tell them that God is your personal stylist. He made you over and gave you this amazing new look. He started with the inside which worked its way to the outside. People may not be receptive at first, but that is okay. You planted a seed by telling someone about the good God has done for you. As you continue to walk with confidence, live in peace, and express joy, they will begin to give some weight to what you said. Soon they will tire of the tapes and classes alone that are not producing the overall results they seek. No matter how attractive, cut, or sexy a person may appear, they can't look the same way you do if they don't have Jesus.

Have you ever met a person that was extremely gorgeous, then after spending time with that person, they were not so attractive? That is because their spirit does not have the beauty of Christ. Similar to a brick front house, new shutters and new landscaping can always be applied, but if the structure is faulty, it can't stand. Like the house, your physical appearance can change as well, but first find contentment in God. Your desires, once based out of insecurity, may change as well. If not, you will be able to pursue a healthy, wholesome look with God as your coach.

The new look you desire to see may not appear overnight. Yes, Jesus comes into your life and makes you a new as soon as you accept him. But it may take a while for your eyes and your mind to adjust to the new you. Make it a part of your daily confession, "I am beautiful, I am wonderful, I am perfectly made. I am the image of God on earth, and I know it!" Psalms 139: 13—14 says,

> "*[13] For you created my inmost being; you knit me together in my mother's womb. [14] I praise you because I am fearfully and wonderfully made; your works are wonderful, I know that full well.*" NIV

As you begin to speak to your image, what you see as your reflection will be just as God sees you. The beauty on the outside can't compare to the transformation that happens within.

chapter 4

One Size Fits All

OUTWARD APPEARANCES TRULY reflect inner beauty. And because what we look like says something about who we are, what we believe, and what is important, women in particular spend time on making sure their appearance is as flawless as possible. We scan through the closet racks until we find the perfect outfit to wear. We accessorize with matching shoes, handbags and jewelry. A touch of color is added to the face and nails. When we're all done, we take a look at the finished product in a full length mirror, turning from side to side, examining every angle. Once you get a good looking woman in front of the mirror, it's hard to get her to walk away. It's almost as difficult as trying to get a bride to take off her wedding dress. She won't leave until she is confident that her look is complete, the best it's going to get.

The problem with appearances is that they can be deceiving, what looks good on one minute, doesn't look so great the next. So, we switch it up. Red use to be the color to wear; now you're on binge for blue. You try different styles, patterns colors, but something is still missing.

The mind can play tricks on us if it has not been renewed. What we think looks good one minute, may not be the best possible look we need for the next. Certainly making the decision on what to wear can be time consuming, frustrating, and tiresome. Everything you have in your current wardrobe isn't cutting it. You need something fresh, something new, something that will leave a lasting impression. Many times we avoid trying something new. We put an outfit on for a few seconds and take it right off because we are worried that the perceived change will be too drastic. We become skeptics. This really doesn't look that great. What if someone else is wearing the same thing? Every excuse is made to get us to change our minds about the decision. It's challenging at times to get people, even ourselves, to believe in something that seems too good to be true.

Think about those pieces of clothing that are advertised as "one size fits all." Skepticism is typically associated with that claim. Is this really going to work? It has to be a scam. How can one size fit every man, woman, and child? It's impossible. If it contains that much spandex, I am not sure I want it. How good can it really look on? It will either be too tight, too loose, too short, or too long.

With most "one size fit all" apparel, people don't know whether it will work or not until they try it. Many completely shy away because they were not willing to invest the time and resource to see if it really worked. It is those who walk away that miss out when the claim is proven to be true.

The same skepticism associated with the "one size fits all" claim and finding the best look for you is also evident when it comes to Jesus.

"I'm not so sure this is going to work for me."

"He might look good on that person, but he won't fit well in my life."

"Okay, I'll try him for a little while but soon He will become uncomfortable and I going to have to take Him off."

"I wouldn't be caught dead wearing Him; what would people say?"

"You do you, but I am going to stick to my life."

You are partly right if you think you wouldn't be caught dead in him. At that point, you would have rejected Christ. The sinful life you chose to wear will be the one that you sport for eternity in the lake of fire. And you thought your life was so hot while on earth. The match seems suiting.

People are deceived if they think Jesus doesn't look good on. What! When is the last time you looked in the mirror? The Lord is striking. He is the most attractive look you could ever have. He is even versatile. No matter the occasion, casual or formal, He fits them all. Don't let the advertisements fool you; suiting up in God's dress causes every head to turn. When Jesus road into Jerusalem a few days before the Passover, there was so much excitement,

> "[10]*when Jesus entered Jerusalem, the whole city was stirred and asked, "Who is this?"* [11]*The crowds answered, "This is Jesus, the prophet from Nazareth in Galilee."*
> Matthew 21:10-11 NIV

Those who didn't know who Jesus was became well informed by those who did. It is almost a surprise that everyone didn't know Jesus was coming to town; the Holy Spirit commands attention. He draws people into Him. Once you have accepted Christ, the same spirit that was on Jesus now lives in you. Thus, people will begin to take notice. Everywhere you walk, a head will turn. People who knew you before will take a second look. *"Have you seen so and so? There is something different about her. She has a glow that radiates and peaceful nature about her."* The difference they see but may not be able to name is the Holy Spirit.

The Holy Sprit living on the inside causes a change to take place. Like someone who was blue in the face from death, the color of Christ flushes your face as you are washed clean by His blood that was shed. You are revitalized and empowered to do all that you could not do before. When the Holy Spirit came upon Jesus, Jesus was able to perform miraculous works.

"37You know what has happened throughout Judea, beginning in Galilee after the baptism that John preached—38how God anointed Jesus of Nazareth with the Holy Spirit and power, and how he went around doing good and healing all who were under the power of the devil, because God was with him"
Acts 10:37-38 NIV

Once again, the business is buzzing about Jesus. People are discussing what wondrous acts he performed because of the power that was working in Him.

Don't be surprised when people disperse quickly when you walk into the break room. Your spirit is the topic of conversation. They are trying to figure out how you got that promotion when you haven't been at the company for a year. They want to understand where the car that sits in your designated parking spot came from. How is it that she just closed on a five-hundred thousand dollar home? They heard that your family was breaking up but is now happier than ever.

The upgrades apparent in your life are a result of the presence of the Holy Spirit. This is because the Holy Spirit induces a chemical change. He alters the composition of a person. One bond is broken and another forged. Similar to when two hydrogen molecules combine with one oxygen molecule, water is made. What was before is no more. The nature of sin that permeated every area of life is dispelled. The flesh no longer craves the things that use to satisfy. The Spirit desires a life pleasing unto

Christ. The walk, talk, and demeanor will be so substantially different that the smell of sin is ad nauseum. Psalms 34:8 challenges us to take a bite, experience Him with all of our senses to discover He is good. After trying Jesus, you won't want to put on anything else. There is an immediate addiction to spending time in His word, basking in His presence, enjoying the benefits of His love. There is nothing else in the world, no job or person, that can compare to the level of satisfaction Jesus brings.

With the changing of self come new abilities, like a superhero. Before the power kicked in, you were a regular person working a nine to five job. With Christ you have amazing abilities. You can move mountains with your words, believe for something and it appears, and defeat foes without fighting a battle. There is a supernatural ability. As the Luke 1:37 says,

"[37]For with God nothing shall be impossible."

Having the Holy Spirit ever-present is not solely about obtaining victories you were unable to before. When He enters your life, He also brings wholeness and restoration. Any area that was broken before, the Holy Spirit fixes. If wounds remain from battle, He heals them.

If you have ever witnessed or experienced a car crash, after the accident there is glass and debris everywhere. So much debris is scattered that the lanes of the road are closed because they are no longer safe to travel. Emergency response arrives on the scene to get the mangled vehicle cleared from the road and the traffic moving again.

There are times when we have colliding events that leave a great deal of debris. The event was so traumatic that you can't navigate through a normal day, everything stops. The Holy Spirit is the emergency response that comes to clear away all the hurt and painful memories blocking you from moving forward. He has such an amazing power to remove all of the debris in your life, you can't even tell something devastating happened. Romans 15:13 says God pours so much joy and peace into you that it overflows by the power of the Holy Spirit. Having the Holy Spirit indwelling in you is a blessing or empowerment from the Lord. It works in you, on you, and all around you. The spirit of the Lord is able to move on our behalves because we cover ourselves with Him.

When we wake up each morning, we dress ourselves. Minimally, we put on undergarments, a blouse, slacks, socks and shoes. Though some would prefer to walk around as free as the wind, we clothe ourselves to protect our bodies from the outside elements and arrest for indecent exposure. The same way we clothe our physical bodies, putting on the right sock, then the left, is the same way we should dress our spirit. Ephesians 6:11-18 says to,

> "*11Put on the whole armour of God, that ye may be able to stand against the wiles of the devil. 12For we wrestle not against flesh and blood, but against principalities, against powers, against the rulers of the darkness of this world,*

against spiritual wickedness in high places. [13]Wherefore take unto you the whole armour of God, that ye may be able to withstand in the evil day, and having done all, to stand. [14]Stand therefore, having your loins girt about with truth, and having on the breastplate of righteousness; [15]And your feet shod with the preparation of the gospel of peace; [16]Above all, taking the shield of faith, wherewith ye shall be able to quench all the fiery darts of the wicked. [17]And take the helmet of salvation, and the sword of the Spirit, which is the word of God: [18]Praying always with all prayer and supplication in the Spirit, and watching thereunto with all perseverance and supplication for all saints;"

The enemy is going to attack you. He knows you are a woman of purpose and have kingdom business to handle. He will stop at nothing to ruin you. What starts as a mere snag runs all the way through your life and now you are in a place you did not intend to be. The Father gives us the ability to stand against enemy. We hold up our lives with truth, strap that righteousness to our cheats and put on those pumps of peace. The bag we tote with our daily essentials is the one of faith. When we see a wrinkle coming, we remove the static with our travel size spray. That zipper can't break because we have a safety pin in our possession. With every attack, we have something in our handbag of faith to fight back. Adorn your head with salvation and gloss those lips with the word of God. As you have topped off the spiritual dress for the day, pray, and know nothing can touch you.

Before you dressed your life with Christ, you had a "good side," a certain angle that you preferred to be viewed from. Every picture you took always had the same pose. There were certain outfits you wore, absolutely nothing too fitting because you didn't want those "problem areas" to show. Once you put on the Holy Spirit, the 360 degree view becomes flawless. There is no excess hanging anywhere. You no longer have to be embarrassed by the sinful problem areas. All of the past is gone and the Holy Spirit is left to amplify the best new you. Please believe the hype. God truly is "One size fits all."

chapter 5

Pick a Color

EVEN AFTER ACCEPTING Christ and being transformed inside and out by His word, a spiritual battle continues to wage for your soul. Those bad hair days aren't just a coincidence; they are attacks to get you off of your best game and deter you from walking with Christ.

Have you ever felt blue? How about green with envy? Has there been a time when you were so livid that you saw red? If you took a peak at your emotions, what would you find? It is natural to have feelings and to express those feelings; but do the emotions experienced daily align with the word of God? We have to evaluate our color spectrum and make sure that all the variations of emotions come from the three primary colors, God the Father, God the Son, and God the Holy Spirit.

We know that when God created us, He made us in His image. That didn't just include our outwardly, physical appearance, but our spiritual makeup as well. God is a God of love and compassion. He is a God of joy and happiness. He gave us emotions so that we could relate to Him and to those around us. However, sin pollutes our nature and is accompanied by an ensemble of ungodly feelings. Galatians 5: 19—23 says,

> "[19]*The acts of the sinful nature are obvious: sexual immorality, impurity and debauchery;* [20]*idolatry and witchcraft; hatred, discord, jealousy, fits of rage, selfish ambition, dissensions, factions* [21]*and envy; drunkenness, orgies, and the like. I warn you, as I did before, that those who live like this will not inherit the kingdom of God .* [22]*But the fruit of the Spirit is love, joy, peace, patience, kindness, goodness, faithfulness,* [23]*gentleness and self-control. Against such things there is no law.*" NIV

When we give our lives to Christ, we close our hearts on the sinful nature and shut out anger, hatred, jealousy, selfishness, envy, fighting, and drunken partying. We then choose to worship God only, partying with Jesus, and enjoy the pleasantries of the spirit. Because we belong to Christ and walk in stride with the Holy Spirit, we can feel good all the time. That isn't to say that your environment will not be chaotic occasionally and that people won't behave in a way that would ordinarily get on your nerves; but it is completely possible to operate in peace and contentment when relationships, finances, or work are in temporary disarray. You can still love and pray for the person who lied on you. The actions that once induced rage and a severe tongue lashing will roll off your shoulders with ease. It is possible not to be hardened from painful experiences but to be kind and patient as if you were never mistreated. The Holy Spirit makes the seemingly impossible, possible.

> "*⁸Formerly, when you did not know God, you were slaves to those who by nature are not gods. ⁹But now that you know God—or rather are known by God—how is it that you are turning back to those weak and miserable principles? Do you wish to be enslaved by them all over again?*"
> Galatians 4: 8-9 NIV

Sometimes the enemy tries to deceive and disrupt our walk with God by presenting a bag of emotions as if it were from the one who made us. He will offer substitutes for what is good and from God. At times it is very easy to identify the imposter bag, while others may be a bit more difficult. Take for example, a saved woman who is walking with God and waiting for her future husband. During her season of waiting, the enemy introduces concepts of premarital sex subtly through friends and media outlets. She doesn't realize that because she is not guarding what is coming into her heart through her eyes and ears, she is being enticed to open the door and allow sin to come in.

As the woman approaches thirty, her favorite talk show host tells her that she is getting too old to be single. She should accentuate her curves with revealing clothing and behave flirtatiously to attract a man, irrespective of marital status. The woman begins to lust after any man that gives her attention and she falls into sexual sin as a means to hold onto the man of the moment. It isn't until the relationship does not produce a ring or bear any of fruit, that she realizes she was swindled. She was lured into lust rather than enjoying God's love and waiting on the love of her future husband. The initial feelings of excitement, desire, and pleasure quickly fade and reveal the true nature of sin which is disappointment, frustration, and brokenness. Unlike the mirage of sin, what you see is what you get with the Holy Spirit. You will consistently experience God's love, joy and peace as you walk with Him. Even if you stumble, He is always waiting with open arms for you to return.

Along with His unfailing love, God is a God of forward progression. He doesn't stall or reverse into your past. Whatever has been done by you and to you is forgiven. He only moves forward. The enemy will come however to poison the mind and emotions by saying, *"God is driving too slowly. You will never reach your desired destination. Your beat up car couldn't make it even with the Lord's help,"* he will boldly lie. Like a deceitful tour guide, the enemy will do anything to compel you to take the drivers seat and put God on the passenger side, or kick Him out all together. The destination of fulfillment and prosperity God was taking you to will be completely out of sight before you know it because you followed the enemy's directions. Satin is clueless when it comes to the blessings of the Lord. He couldn't tell you the first thing about how to get to what God has for you. He can only furnish a one way ticket or roadmap to the same place he is, eternal damnation and separation from God.

The first few stops with him as your navigator may seem fun, partying all night long, idolizing possessions and money, having intimate relationships with someone who you are not married to. Then the scenic route becomes drearier and less scenic. Because you have not arrived at the place God called you to be, depression, anxiety, or anger sets in. Your tank is always on empty and no matter what you try, outside of God, you are never completely satisfied. The sin begins to mount and weigh you down. The mistakes drive you into a state of depression. You sit at home singing sad songs, living in regret, feeling sorry for yourself. Everyday you knock off a pint of rocky road ice cream and down a bottle of choice. You can't believe you have sinned so badly against God and now you are living with the consequences of your decisions. Like a disease, the depression progresses. You go from being a little blue to gray, then almost into black, a state of nothingness as you seek to end your life.

The devil is a liar. Put down that spoon and bottle. Substances can't fill you and make the woes go away.

"For the kingdom of God is not a matter of eating and drinking, but of righteousness, peace and joy in the Holy Spirit,"
Romans 14:17 NIV

Pick up the word of God, read your Bible, confess the word, call out to God. Ask Him to wash you clean of sin with the blood of Jesus, which makes your heart and conscious whiter than snow. Kick the devil out and invite

Jesus back into the driver's seat in Jesus' name. The word says that every demon has to flee when the name of Jesus is proclaimed. Speak to the depression and sinful nature feelings. Tell them they have to go, right now! God will immediately restore you and provide victory in the internal battle of emotions.

The key is to not be fooled by the flashy colors of sin that appeal to the lower nature of our being. What is at first blush appealing truly has no substance and weight in the kingdom of God. If the colors of our thoughts, feelings, and emotions do not possess God the Father, the Son, and the Holy Spirit, then we need to pick a color that does.

chapter 6

Odd Math

MASTERING THE COLOR spectrum of emotions and discovering our intricate details is all part of learning what wonderful women we are in Christ. From a very young age we are taught how to read, write, count and reason. We know that things on earth have an order and abide by a modus operandi. What goes up will surely fall to the ground. Everything that begins will at some point come to an end. One plus one is always two. Though we were created by God, His ways of reasoning and mode of operation are outside the bounds of our cognitive ability.

> "*8For my thoughts are not your thoughts, neither are your ways my ways, saith the LORD.*"
> Isaiah 55:8

This means that the little list you carry around in your wallet with characteristics of your husband should be thrown away. God knows us better than we know ourselves. Thus, God needs no direction as to who will be a compatible lifetime partner. He formed you and your spouse in your mother's wombs to fulfill His purpose and each other. The Lord may be so gracious as to grant a few items on the list, but God is certainly a God of surprise. And usually when "the one" shows up, Surprise!

Most married women will tell you that the love of their life doesn't closely resemble the person they dreamed of since they were thirteen. The tall, dark and handsome man may actually be short, red, and adorable. The doctor from Washington D.C. may be the school teacher from Wisconsin. It's true that there are certain physical characteristics that attract women to the opposite sex. The enjoyment of common activities is even a plus. With time, the physical appearance changes and as your marriage progresses, you begin to love one another's hobbies. What is most important in the connection two individuals have with each other is the connection they have individually with God. Their spirit calls out to yours in a way no physical attraction or other commonality can.

In First Samuel 16, the Lord sends his servant Samuel to a town called Bethlehem. Saul was currently king of Israel but had disobeyed God and lost the Lord's trust. As a result, Samuel was ordered to find a replacement king. Samuel did as he was told by the Lord. When he arrived in Bethlehem, he immediately saw "the one."

"When they arrived, Samuel saw Eliab and thought, "Surely the LORD's anointed stands here before the LORD." [7] But the LORD said to Samuel, "Do not consider his ap-

pearance or his height, for I have rejected him. The LORD does not look at the things man looks at. Man looks at the outward appearance, but the LORD looks at the heart." ⁸ *Then Jesse called Abinadab and had him pass in front of Samuel. But Samuel said, "The LORD has not chosen this one either."* ⁹ *Jesse then had Shammah pass by, but Samuel said, "Nor has the LORD chosen this one."* ¹⁰ *Jesse had seven of his sons pass before Samuel, but Samuel said to him, "The LORD has not chosen these."*
I Samuel 16:6-10 NIV

The courting process can be long and tiresome. You've gone on dates with men that run the spectrum, those met at the gym or at the super market. You humored your mother and went out with the young man on her job. You even tried speed dating. In each situation, the men were evaluated against a list and determined to be "In" or "Out."

Dating without God's direction is like throwing darts at a target blindfolded. We choose to keep throwing darts hoping to hit something, anything. We trust in everyone else's opinion of who would be great for us rather than asking the one who has the definitive answer. Just like Samuel, the one you are so sure of, the one that fits the bill, may not be the one God has chosen. He knows what makes us happy and what grieves us. He is aware of every choice we will make. And as we are purposed by God to be our husband's helpers, God knows who we can best lend a helping hand to.

In the process of waiting for mister right to show up, seek God. Trust that He will reveal His best to you. Women often say, "*I am worth the wait*," and we are. But if we get tired of waiting, the worth goes out the window and we marry the next one through the door. Whatever biological time clock you are running on, take out the batteries. God operates outside of time. Don't become discouraged and make a selection out of haste. Samuel knew that there had to be more sons than the ones he already saw. He was not going to bring back another. Another was not called to be the king of Israel . No matter how long it took, he was going to be patient until he found the king God sent him to find.

> "*So he asked Jesse, "Are these all the sons you have?"*
> "*There is still the youngest," Jesse answered, "but he is tending the sheep."*
> *Samuel said, "Send for him; we will not sit down* [a] *until he arrives."* [12] *So he sent and had him brought in. He was ruddy, with a fine appearance and handsome features. Then the LORD said, "Rise and anoint him; he is the one."*
> I Samuel 16:11-12 NIV

Samuel's endurance paid off. While waiting for the last son, Samuel stood. He was not going to sit down and get too comfortable because he was expecting "the one" to walk through the door. During your single season, prepare yourself for your husband. Take the time to grow spiritually and understand what God desires from a wife. Avoid developing habits that will not be conducive to a married lifestyle. Whatever you do, don't become complacent; be ready to be swept off of your feet.

Women say all the time, "*there isn't much on the market to choose from, pick one and be happy.*" Where are you shopping? If it's a thrift store, then yes, the selection will be picked over. But the Kingdom of Heaven is top of the line. A lifetime guarantee comes with everything. Consider when you are looking for that one item no store seems to have, you will travel across town to purchase what you can not live without. You will call in advance to make sure it is there. You will even ask the store manager to help you comb through the isles because you are not leaving the store without it. If you have that much determination over a material object, certainly you can have the same for your husband. Tell God that you are going to wait for him until He brings him out.

When it came to finding the new king of Israel, no moment was spared once David came through the door. He was the one God had chosen. The Lord told Samuel, "He is the one." Then He said to bring him up and anoint him. When God brings you "the one," that is not the time to play hard to get. Take hold of what God has given you. Taking hold to your man is not the same as being intimate with him. That is the world's view of how to get and keep a man, which is false. Having sex with someone does not guarantee a wedding date. If it did, people would marry the first person they were willingly intimate with. The physical exploration of a man and woman were designed to be performed within the marital context.

Intimacy before marriage creates a plethora of complications due to the nature of sin. Someone's heart may be broken because the expectation of commitment was not met. A disease could become the ring and constant reminder that the intimate union took place. Or a child could result. All children are blessings from God. Not one is a mistake. But now, either the man or the woman has to perform a role they were not designed to because the other partner isn't around.

After God introduces you to your future husband, this is the time that you get to know him as a person, his likes and dislikes, dreams and goals. At some point he will pop the big question. How do you know he will ask you? Because God told you, "he is the one." So when he asks, say yes. God has already given the stamp of approval, what your girlfriends have to say really doesn't matter, nor does anyone else.

> "⁶*But at the beginning of creation God 'made them male and female.*'[a] ⁷'*For this reason a man will leave his father and mother and be united to his wife,*[b] ⁸*and the two will become one flesh.*'[c] *So they are no longer two, but one.*"
> Mark 10:6-8 NIV

The principles of addition you learned in pre-K where one plus one equals two should be disregarded when it comes to marriage. Marriage is a union between husband, wife, and the trinity, God the father, God the son, and God the Holy Spirit. When you add all required parties, the solution is always one. You and your husband are one in spirit with Christ. Your individual characteristics will persist, but no longer will you operate as separate entities.

Any other person attached to the marriage covenant violates the principle of being one. Principles of division and subtraction will begin to operate. Bad advice and outside influence can reduce the value of the relationship or take away time and energy until there is little left for the marriage. The connection between man and woman is so strong that the Bible says a man will leave the only family he has known, the people who loved him and cared for him his entire life, and come into union with a woman. He maintains a relationship with his family but man now takes responsibility for the treatment and care of his new wife. She is his first priority, an order of operations exist. The husband submits to God. The wife submits to the husband; and children submit to both patents.

There are rules in math that provide guidelines of how to obtain the correct answer when the problem has more than one operational sign. Anything inside the parenthesis should be tackled first. Every financial and emotional need within your household comes first. The outside exponents come after the inside is taken care of. The next operation is multiplication. God will keep his promise to multiply. You are to be a good steward, an adequate devisor of resources for those people and opportunities he so chooses to add and subtract from your life. Just as in math, if the order is violated, the answer will always come out wrong. You'll get an answer but it won't be God's answer. The one you have might work for a while but before long, evidence of the miscalculation will become apparent. You will begin to see that the marriage is unbalanced. Your life that once made perfect sense no longer adds up. Choosing to Operate in God's order always produces the desired result.

Husband + Wife = One in Christ

chapter 7

Baggage Free

I Do! Kiss, kiss, kiss. The rice is thrown, the broom jumped, and the cake cut. The couple rushes off to enjoy a magical celebration of their unity and then returns home. The only things they should have with them are lots of pictures, souvenirs, stories, and of course Jesus. Sometimes when the bride and groom are whisked away from the wedding, the luggage for their vacation isn't the only baggage they carry. Lofty suitcases and duffle bags of sorrow are often carried forward into the marriage.

We have to be mindful not to allow past experiences to negatively impact forward progression. Like a reoccurring cold, a past pain can cause your present to become sick. And though the body has a defense system to ward away bad bugs, it wasn't designed to be exposed to a harmful virus on a continual basis.

The average Fahrenheit temperature of a human body is Ninety-eight point six degrees, plus or minus a degree in either direction. If a temperature rises above 100 degrees, the person has a fever. If a temperature falls below 86 degrees, that person is extremely ill. A shift in body temperature is usually a good indicator that something is wrong.

Events in life have the potential to trigger a temperature change. They can cause your blood to boil, head to steam, eyes to water, and ears to burn with rage. A depression so severe can set in that the body becomes cold and rigid. With either extreme, the body can not sustain its normal functionality because it was designed to be 98.6°.

I don't know anyone who enjoys being sick. Who would actually inhale the cough of neighbor? Have you witnessed someone who deliberately touches every place a sick person touched and wipes his or her face with a used tissue? Who uses the same toothbrush as someone with strep throat? The answer is the person who wants to be and stay sick. For whatever reason, that person enjoys not coming out of the house. She would rather be isolated and quarantined to her given quarters. She doesn't want to let anyone into her life. She is prepared to be alone and ultimately die the same way.

The baggage we carry from past experiences are like a reoccurring virus. Once it looks to be all better, something happens and the symptoms come rushing back. Instead of washing our hands, throwing away the old toothbrush, or taking cough medicine, we allow the things of old to penetrate our current, healthy state and bring us back to a place of sickness, disease, and death. This is not to say that there won't be instances in life when old memories surface. It is what we do with the old memories, past pain, and former behavior that makes the difference.

In Genesis chapters 18 and 19, we are introduced to two cities by the name of Sodom and Gomorrah . Both cities were filled with wicked men. They had no regard for the Lord and sinned greatly against Him. The Lord told His faithful servant Abraham that because of the overwhelming sin in Sodom, God was going to destroy the city. However, Abraham's nephew Lot lived in Sodom . So Abraham asked the Lord to save the city if God could find ten righteous people there. Because of His merciful nature, He granted Abraham's request. Two angels of the Lord went to Sodom and were greeted by Lot.

Lot knew that the city was full of vile men who sought to defile all that was righteous. Having this knowledge, Lot insisted that the angles stay at his dwelling. Despite his effort, the wicked men continued to seek out the righteous.

> "12 *The two men said to Lot, "Do you have anyone else here—sons-in-law, sons or daughters, or anyone else in the city who belongs to you? Get them out of here,* 13 *because we are going to destroy this place. The outcry to the LORD against its people is so great that he has sent us to destroy it."* 14 *So Lot went out and spoke to his sons-in-law, who were pledged to marry* [a] *his daughters. He said, "Hurry and get out of this place, because the LORD is about to destroy the city!" But his sons-in-law thought he was joking.*

[15] With the coming of dawn, the angels urged Lot, saying, "Hurry! Take your wife and your two daughters who are here, or you will be swept away when the city is punished." [16] When he hesitated, the men grasped his hand and the hands of his wife and of his two daughters and led them safely out of the city, for the LORD was merciful to them. [17] As soon as they had brought them out, one of them said, "Flee for your lives! Don't look back, and don't stop anywhere in the plain! Flee to the mountains or you will be swept away!"
Genesis 19:12-17 NIV

God is merciful. He brings us through difficulty and trials in our lives. All that surrounds us may be in disarray but God doesn't allow us to be swallowed by circumstance. He gives direction of how to get away from trouble or people who wish us no good. Destruction can't take place until you reach a point of safety.

There are moments in your deliverance when you can try to help someone else. The difficulty experienced may be used as a testimony that inspires change in someone else's life. The two of you can come out of the thing together. When Lot told his son-in-laws that destruction was coming and they couldn't stay in the same place, they laughed at him. Sometimes people are not willing or ready to change. They don't take the dire situation seriously or you for that matter. At that point you have to keep moving. You shared the word from the Lord, what they do with it is between them and God. Your first responsibility is to get out.

Sometimes on the way to recovery, relapses occur. We expose ourselves to the same bug that made us sick from the beginning. When a woman is recovering from drug addiction or alcoholism, she can not continue to surround herself with people that partake in the activities she is recovering from. Yes, she has the grace of God on her life and spirit of healing but staying in the same environment can delay her progress and cause her to never make it out of the place that will ultimately destroy her.

Sometimes women in a continuously abusive relationship miss the voice of God when He says it's time to leave. She prayed for him, sought counseling, and witnessed the word of the Lord, but he would not change and turn his heart to God. She mistakenly puts her hope in someone other than God and trusts that man alone can change his sinful ways.

"*He will change*," she thinks.

"*This won't happen again.*"

"*It's my fault; I can handle it.*"

She doesn't realize that everything that concerns her concerns God. He alone has the power to change a situation and handle any matter. Sometimes men refuse to listen and obey the voice of the Lord. In the Book of Exodus, Moses was sent by God to order the release of the Israelites from slavery. Pharaoh was told on more than one occasion to let the Israelites go. But Pharaoh refused to do God's bidding. Plague after plague struck Egypt until Pharaoh did as God commanded.

Prior to the release, God prepared His people. He told them to get ready, suit up, and pack their belongings because deliverance was near. Though the Israelites had been in bondage for 400 years, they were not to be afraid; God would be with them.

Because God knows the end from beginning, He knows if a man will turn his heart to Him. He knows if a man will never abuse a woman again. God has details on the new love and reverence for God the couple will share. God is also cognizant of those who do not know Him and those who refuse to accept Him. When man hardens his heart like Pharaoh, God moves to protect His beloved. Like with the children of Israel, God at times has to say, "Get ready, it's time to be free from bondage." Though coming out of Egypt may seem frightening, fear is not associated with the Holy Spirit. God has given the power, mind, and love for self to leave an abusive relationship. You are too important to God to stay if He says it's time to go.

Consider the functionality of traffic lights. They are designed to direct the flow of traffic. A red light means stop, stay right where you are. Things are moving on the other side. Yellow means slow down, be cautions. A change is about to occur that will affect your lane. When you see a green light, you are free to move forward.

God directs the traffic in your life as well. He tells you when to stop, when to stay right where you are. He is moving on the other side and changing the environment so you can move forward again. He also provides warning. Take caution, pay attention, a change is coming. Finally, God lets you know when it is time to go. When He gives the green light, be confident that the intersection is clear and it is safe to move forward. If you sit in neutral, ignore the green light, or start to go and stop in the intersection, you may put yourself in dangerous situation. Someone could run right into you and three things could happen. The wreck may just rattle you a little. It could result in injury. Or there is also that horrible possibility that the accident could claim your life. If and when God says go, go!

Just like children don't always heed their parents' warnings, sometimes we dismiss the warning of God. He has given us instruction over and over and we don't listen. Take two teaspoons twice a day for a week and you will see results. It might not taste good, but the road to recovery will be brief and superior health long-lasting. You take the first few doses and stop; or you just stare at the bottle all week and not take one at all. The key to recovery is sitting on your counter but you refuse to follow the instructions. You hesitated just like Lot. *"If I take it, am I really going to feel better?"* *"Maybe things will change on their own."* So eventually God takes you by the hand and leads you out. He won't let you stay where you are. You are too precious to him. Daddy picks up that spoon, pours a dose of His medicine, and says, "Open wide; you are going to get better." Then God heals and delivers.

Being healed doesn't mean that the sickness or injury never occurred. It doesn't mean that you weren't wounded deeply. It simply means that you are no longer inflicted with pain and suffering. If you have ever had an operation, no matter how skilled the surgeon, you probably have a tiny scar. Though you no longer are in bondage to the infirmity, there is a small reminder that you were hurt at some point. The scar is tied to a memory, which is tied to emotion, which can then alter behavior. One glance at the scar can trigger a spiraling of downward events. Before long, you are depressed, angry, or revengeful. These emotions are then transferred to the people around you and they too are affected by the scar.

After Lot left Sodom with his wife and daughters, he reached safety as God promised. But Lot's wife disobeyed the angels of the Lord. They told the family not to look back.

> "25 *Thus he overthrew those cities and the entire plain, including all those living in the cities—and also the vegetation in the land.* 26 *But Lot's wife looked back, and she became a pillar of salt.*"
> Genesis 19:25-26 NIV

Because Lot's wife looked back into her past, she was trapped there. Everyone else could move on, but she became stuck right outside the place God delivered her from. As the Lord delivers you, He reconstructs your life. When He is finished, there is no more pain. You may still have a memory but the nerve endings in that memory are severed. If you reflect long enough on painful memories from the past, they will inhibit your ability to move forward to create and enjoy new ones.

As relationships are forged between a man and a woman, each party decides what belongings they will ultimately bring into the marriage. He wants to bring his big, black, leather sofa and she wants to display a large collection of porcelain Dalmatians. The couple sifts through their belongings and determines what will best suit their lifestyle together. Each piece of furniture is arranged nicely in their new home. A problem doesn't surface until one spouse finds that the other brought something with them they agreed not to.

When God called Abram, He gave specific instructions that were tied to a promise. God told Abram to leave his country and the member's of his father's household. God would then bless Abram abundantly. So Abram did as God commanded, partially. He left but he took his nephew Lot with him. Though God has a great plan for us, we have to participate to receive. We can't half step. We follow step one and two, skip three, half way complete four, finish five, and then we're done. Abram did increase abundantly but soon there became little room for all of his and Lot's possessions together. So a quarrel broke out between them and they had to separate.

"Now Lot, who was moving about with Abram, also had flocks and herds and tents. [6] But the land could not support them while they stayed together, for their possessions were so great that they were not able to stay together. [7] And quarreling arose between Abram's herdsmen and the herdsmen of Lot. The Canaanites and Perizzites were also living in the land at that time. [8] So Abram said to Lot, "Let's not have any quarreling between you and me, or between your herdsmen and mine, for we are brothers. [9] Is not the whole land before you? Let's part company. If you go to the left, I'll go to the right; if you go to the right, I'll go to the left."
Genesis 13:5-9 NIV

Jesus came to save and to restore. He clears all the junk out of your life so you won't go from place to place carrying stuff you don't need. When God brings a husband and wife together, he instructs the two to leave all the excess baggage behind and become one. It doesn't matter if you dated a man before and he treated you poorly. That doesn't mean that your God fearing husband is going to treat you the same. Your father divorced your mother and left her with three children. So now you don't want kids and are waiting for your husband to pack up and leave. You followed part of God's instruction when you made the marriage commitment but you didn't leave all the excess baggage behind.

Trip advisors will tell you to only pack necessities. Anything else needed, can be obtained along the way. The more you pack into the suitcase, the more you will have to carry and the more it will cost to transport. God has a plan for your life, a journey to embark upon. He tells you what to bring and who should travel with you. Anything else needed on the way, He will provide. You thought you needed to hold onto what your father said. Oh, and you had to carry what the last boyfriend did. Because you took things with you that God intended to remain in the past, your great journey gets interrupted. As you and your spouse grow together, there is no longer room for your false accusations that stem from past relationships. Your marriage can't sustain the defensive attitude your father had toward you mother. All of the crowding causes dissention. The two of you begin to quarrel and ultimately split up.

God said no man should tear apart what He put together. That includes you. It doesn't matter what time of the year it is, do some spring cleaning. Throw out anything that you should have left in the place the Lord brought you from. Disassociate with the people in your life and marriage that shouldn't be there. Once you have eliminated the things that were crowding your space, you will begin to move forward again because there's now room to pick up your blessings at your next stop.

The obstacles we endure in life come from different sources. Because we have the Holy Spirit living on the inside, there is nothing that can not be overcome. Sometimes the lack of forward progression results from the inability to follow God's instruction or let go of the past. Too much clutter takes up space for our blessing. It presents a fire hazard. A tiny spark, acting out on a flicker of a memory, can cause a blaze that can destroy relationships and eliminate opportunity. Stop dragging around junk you don't need. Give it to the Lord. First Peter 5:7 says,

"⁷Casting all your care upon him; for he careth for you."

Now that God holds all of the things that use to weigh you down, you are now free to enjoy the journey with Him.

chapter 8

Home Sweet Home

BEING MARRIED IS such a joy, as is fulfilling any part of God's plan. There are so many nuances that occur. Even if you already did something when you were single, it isn't the same as doing the activity together.

Building your home is one of those memories you'll never forget. From selecting the lot, to picking the carpet, each step is taken with the vision of a dream home in mind. Similar to how a house is built, brick by brick, one decision after the other, so to is the marital relationship. Every event, decision, and moment of communication lays a brick. Each brick has to be laid upon a solid foundation.

Every standing piece of construction needs a solid foundation. When new construction commences, builders pour a layer of concrete to serve as the base on which the home will stand. For a slab, this base has direct contact with the ground. It is the base's job to be a buffer between the weight of the house and the soil beneath. As the ground shifts and the earth settles, the foundation moves with the soil so that the structure it supports does not fall apart. If the foundation was not set properly, however, the home will begin to suffer internal and external damages and can no longer function as it was originally designed. Cracks will appear, doors or windows will cease to open, and part of the house may even sink below the other half of the home. Restoration of the home can't take place without major repairs; and the condition that caused the foundation problem must be remedied to avoid reoccurring damage.

The same is true with the marital relationship. God is to be the foundation. He serves as the buffer between the weight and functionality of the marriage and outside elements.

"When the enemy shall come in like a flood, the Spirit of the LORD shall lift up a standard against him"
Isaiah 59:19

There are times in a marriage when flooding causes issues to surface like the unsettled earth beneath a home. The pouring of rain causes the solid ground to become fluid. With God as the foundation, He is able to move and to adjust with the fluctuations of the soil. We never even feel a thing. No damage is sustained to our dwelling because God is an adequate, superior foundation.

Do you remember the week of your wedding? Things were so hectic. Relatives flew into town from all over the country. The wedding dress had to be altered a second time. The florist got the flu and couldn't make your bouquets. Despite the chaos and obstacles, somehow, you made it to the special day. You stood before God and thanked Him for your spouse by making promises to honor and cherish each other forever, no matter what. After the reception and honeymoon, the dust settled and all that was left and that mattered was you, your spouse, and most importantly, God.

When we say "I do," we make a covenant and decision to begin building. The wedding dress and tuxedo come off and the hardhat and boots are put on. It is at that moment we start to build and pour a foundation. We establish the rules of how the marriage will function, who will write the bills, who will take out the trash, what is and is not important and acceptable to the functionality of our unity. This is a critical time because a decision is made as to what materials will be used. Will the word of God be the underlying layer and point of reference for every decision and action?

Matthew 7:24-27 states,

"*24Therefore whosoever heareth these sayings of mine, and doeth them, I will liken him unto a wise man, which built his house upon a rock: 25And the rain descended, and the floods came, and the winds blew, and beat upon that house; and it fell not: for it was founded upon a rock. 26And every one that heareth these sayings of mine, and doeth them not, shall be likened unto a foolish man, which built his house upon the sand:* [27]*And the rain descended, and the floods came, and the winds blew, and beat upon that house; and it fell: and great was the fall of it."*

There are going to be trials and unexpected events that come and test your marriage. The car may break down, a spouse may loose a job, an unplanned pregnancy occurs, or the children you planned for don't come.

"[7] Since no man knows the future, who can tell him what is to come?" Ecclesiastes 8:7 NIV

Trials face everyone. What makes the difference in the outcome is where the house is built. If you are standing on the word, trusting and believing in God, no hurricane can knock you down. If you have your faith in a company, in an activity, or person, you are going to have a lot of debris to clean after the storm.

Many times we emulate our marriage after our parent's relationship, things we have heard from realities or friends, or what we have seen in movies. We construct our marriage based on a faulty design.

"The person who provides for the family financially is allowed to have an affair."

"So long as the bruises fade by the morning, it's okay."

"I can stay out all night and party if I like because I am going home when the bar closes."

"I have a year to test this marriage thing out. If I don't like it, it can be annulled, divorce if I have to."

"This is the twenty-first century. He can cook his own food and wash his own underwear."

We get these ideas in our head of how the marriage is to be structured that have **nothing** to do with God's intent for marriage.

Because of God's nature, He gave man freewill, the power to choose one's words and actions. But He also provides advise that if followed would lead us to Him and the good life He intended. God specifically cautions about building a life outside of His word. First Corinthians 3:10- 15 warns,

> *"[10]By the grace God has given me, I laid a foundation as an expert builder, and someone else is building on it. But each one should be careful how he builds. [11]For no one can lay any foundation other than the one already laid, which is Jesus Christ. [12]If any man builds on this foundation using gold, silver, costly stones, wood, hay or straw, [13]his work will be shown for what it is, because the Day will bring it to light. It will be revealed with fire, and the fire will test the quality of each man's work. [14]If what he has built survives, he will receive his reward. [15]If it is burned up, he will suffer loss; he himself will be saved, but only as one escaping through the flames."* NIV

Sometimes we meet a person and are attracted to their sexy physique, large bank account, or socio-economic status. We overlook the fact that the person does not know Christ.

"He can get to know him, right?"

"He may be married but he really doesn't love his wife; he'll be a better husband to me."

The marriage is then built outside of Christ. There are instances when both spouses know Christ but do not invite God into their daily walk. They plan to have 3.5 kids in seven years, a house, and make partner in a law firm by the age of forty. Is that what God had planned for your life? You may be happy for a while, but there is no joy like the one experienced when fulfilling God's plan for you.

"Many are the plans in a man's heart, but it is the LORD's purpose that prevails,"
Proverbs 19:21 NIV

So what happens? The paint begins to peel first. He isn't as nice of a guy as you thought he was. The money in the account wasn't earned honestly. The car he drives is leased and home rented. You can't pray when your spouse is around. The plan you had for 3.5 kids, house and the whole shebang is shot. Your husband can not physically have children of his own, the dream neighborhood is in a flood zone, and you hate practicing law. The attention received as the secondary wife is now going to another secondary with your promotion to primary. The relationship you worked so hard to build and care for is now in shambles.

It's okay if you find yourself in a nightmare rather than the dream you had on your wedding day. God is the master of building and rebuilding. Whatever state your construction is in now, God can remove the caution tape, eliminate all code violations, and make your dwelling safe and enjoyable for living. If you are in a position of having to rebuild, do so with the knowledge and wisdom of God. It is not too late to change the structure of your house now that you are remodeling with Jesus. Colossians 3:18–24 outlines the way in which we should structure our home.

> "*18Wives, submit to your husbands, as is fitting in the Lord. 19Husbands, love your wives and do not be harsh with them. 20Children, obey your parents in everything, for this pleases the Lord. 21Fathers, do not embitter your children, or they will become discouraged. 22Slaves, obey your earthly masters in everything; and do it, not only when their eye is on you and to win their favor, but with sincerity of heart and reverence for the Lord. 23Whatever you do, work at it with all your heart, as working for the Lord, not for men, 24since you know that you will receive an inheritance from the Lord as a reward. It is the Lord Christ you are serving.*" NIV

The word says that wives are to submit themselves to their husbands, understanding that their husbands are submitting themselves to God. Alter the mindset that you are not in control of your life. God is in control. He can do a better job than any of us. Trust that He will guide your family's footsteps. If your spouse is not a believer not or operating under God's principles, pray. Prayer is certain to change things.

God also commands for husbands to take care of their wives. Husbands should not mistreat them, neglect them, speak cruelly to them, or hit them. If your house has any of those characteristics, it is outside the will of God. Know that God loves you and He intends for you to be loved as sincerely by your husband.

I know at some point you have seen children in the store, in restaurants, or possibly in your home that run amuck. They speak disrespectfully to their parents and disobey specific instruction. There appears to be a constant battle of power between the parents and the children. This is because the tiny temper tantrums were never checked and they grew into an out and out rebellion. The jury should not be deciding who will prevail. Parents have authority over their children and it is their God given responsibility to train them in God's ways. Proverbs 19:18 tell us to discipline our children; if we don't, then we are an accomplice to their demise.

"*18Chasten thy son while there is hope, and let not thy soul spare for his crying.*"

If a child doesn't learn how to listen to the first figures of authority in their lives, then how will they learn to listen and submit to the authority of teachers, employers, civil authorities, or God? Children are like sponges, they soak up everything in their environment. Are you teaching your children to be honest, forgiving, and loving? Are you teaching them that there are boundaries and that they can't have things outside of its season? Are you teaching them the word of the Lord? God's nature is peace. Thus, teaching and abiding by His word will bring peace into your home as well as bring favor and blessing to your children.

Irrespective of your household loyalty as a Buckeye or Wolverine fan, parents are their children's biggest fans and greatest supporters. We have the job of training them and getting them ready for the game of life. Some practices will be easy and some will require more effort. But we give them the tools and opportunities they need for the journey ahead.

Most who are avid fans of some sport have an expectation prior to every game that their team is going to win. It doesn't matter if the team is trailing by a few points, we have faith that they will be victorious. Too much has been invested to pack up the seat cushion and umbrella and walk away. Our faces are painted, voices strained, and hearts steadfast on a win.

God tells us to not embitter our children. We are to lift them up and encourage them by our continual cheers and support in the stands. God never gives up on us, never stops rooting for us, and we as parents show God's love to our children in the same way.

Colossians 3 also addresses the attitude we should have in our working environments. Each household is structured differently. Some have a parent that stays home while the spouse works and others have both spouses working. This plan may be by default or design. In any event, we work for the Lord. When the alarm clock or cell phone rings at 5:00 A.M. we are rising to worship and work for God, not XYZ Company. The position you hold may not be your dream job but it is the one God has blessed you with for the current season. It brings income into the house and is used to meet the household needs, however deficient you believe it may be. God always provides for us, so be diligent with what you have. Matthew 25:21 shows us that promotion will result when you are faithful with little.

When God blesses you on the first and fifteen of each month, does it seem like the entire check walks straight out of the front door? Sometimes it doesn't even come inside. An unexpected event requires more of your resources than intended. All that remains in your account after bills, daycare, food, and gas is ten dollars to last you the next fifteen days. You pray and live a life pleasing unto God but your pocketbook is always empty. Someone had to have put the wami on you because your resources are too scarce to sustain your lifestyle however lavish or plain it may be. The constant position of not having enough may be a result of commingling God's funds with yours.

We see in Malachi 3:8-12 that there is a portion of your resources that belong to God. When we neglect to give God the tenth of our resources, we put ourselves in a situation where unexpected events can consume our entire check and half of the next. Conversely, if we bring our tithe to the Lord, He will pour out on you and into your bank account so generously that you won't be able to receive all that He has. You were the employee who never received a bonus; suddenly, you get a check for $10,000. The bill that you thought was coming never came, the insurance covered it all. When you go to checkout at the grocery store, the same items you purchased last month are less this month for some reason. The reason is Jehovah Jireh, our provider. Because you gave Him a small portion of what He blessed you with, God protects and increases the rest. Like healthcare, taxes, and 401k deductions that come out of your check automatically each month, take out God's portion first. Give with joy and watch how He pours into your life, finances, and all other areas.

Along with tithing comes savings and responsible use of God's resources. We are to be faithful managers of his funds. When we invest in stocks and bonds, we entrust an investment manager to hold our money and to invest it wisely so that it will multiply. The better our portfolio performs, the more we entrust to our manager. We are mere managers of God's resources. He entrusts us with the responsibility to utilizing His resources adequately so that He can give us more. As we show ourselves faithful, our portfolio of assets will increase. If we are so entangled by debt, then how can we be an immediate blessing to someone else or even to ourselves? If God told you tomorrow to give someone a car or a home because they had no transportation or place to live, you can't do it if your resources were tied up. If He told you to go and pick out the car you want and the home you desire, are you in a position to do so? It is difficult to be a living example of how good God is when we appear to be in a state of struggle just like the next person. God called us to be more than conquers. This means that the spirit of debt and poverty can not defeat us. Don't think it's a battle? Have you ever had to fight on the phone with a bill collector or dual between which bills to pay first. It is a battle that God has given us victory over. Will money rain down from heaven? Possibly. But right now we have the wisdom to turn little into much by applying God's financial principles in our lives.

Ecclesiastes 11:1, 6 show us how to handle God's resources.

"¹Cast your bread upon the waters, for after many days you will find it again. ⁶ Sow your seed in the morning, and at evening let not your hands be idle, for you do not know which will succeed, whether this or that, or whether both will do equally well." NIV

Whatever we give, we will see again. Though it is important to tithe, we should also be a blessing to others in which ever way God leads. We should not wait for the opportune time to move because we may never see that "perfect" opportunity. It is not for us to understand the ground that we are sewing into, only that God will produce fruit from our seed. While are waiting for results, continue to work hard, be responsible, and worship until the seeds planted produce a harvest.

The reason why builders use a blueprint for construction is so that they may have a clear understanding of what materials are required, where they are in the process and how the structure is to look once completed. Someone with twenty-one years of life experience could probably wing it, but they could miss an important step that leads to the entire collapse of the building. God provides us a blueprint of how to structure our households so that they don't fall apart. Marriage and families are designed to last; and God's plan guarantees a way to withstand any storm.

chapter 9

<u>Out of Bounds</u>

WHEN GOD DESIGNED us to be forged with others, He established defining lines and boundaries. Every person has individual boundaries. Boundaries are a means of separation and definition. Both tangible and intangible in nature, they are used to define territory and to allot space. Envision a picture of a triangle and a square. It's easy to see their differences. One has four sides and the other three. They are both distinct shapes, defined by series of connecting lines. It doesn't matter if they become larger or are made smaller; their composition always remains the same. Yes, the differences are quite clear. It is those differences, however, that make them so unique.

A husband and wife for illustration purposes are like the triangle and square. They are two unique individuals that are defined by a series of boundaries. Boundaries can expand as the couple grows together and they can contract on particular issues. The core of who the husband and wife are individually always remains the same.

Problems arise when the triangle attempts to remove a side of the square and the square tries to add one to the triangle. The inherent uniqueness in each is no longer respected. Both spouses are attempting to alter the composition of the other for selfish reasons. The triangle no longer esteems her square; she wants him to be a triangle too. The square needs for her to get with the program and be square just like him.

Boundaries are very important because they establish guidelines to what is and what is not allowed within those confines. When we make the decision to turn away from sin and give our lives to Christ, we remove ourselves from the boundaries of sin and enter the boundaries of light. According to Colossians 3 the boundless confines of sin are: sexual decadence, impurity, lust, evil desires, greed, idolatry, anger, rage, hatred, slander, dirty language and dishonesty. Within the bounds of Christ through the Holy Spirit are: compassion, kindness, gentleness, patience, love, and forgiveness. If we operate by the rules of our defined territory we reap the rewards associated with that boundary. The reward for living a life of sin is death; the reward for living a life devoted to Christ is eternal life.

> *"23For the wages of sin is death; but the gift of God is eternal life through Jesus Christ our Lord."*
> Romans 6:23

The same functionality of rules and boundaries that we see in our spiritual walk is ever-present in marriage.

God clearly stipulates how a husband is to treat his wife and how a wife is to submit to her husband. A wife should expect her husband to treat her kindly, to be gentle with her, and to feed her soul with fortifying words. A husband should expect his wife to respect him, to support him, and to humbly listen to his thoughts. Both would rightfully anticipate faithfulness, honesty, and compassion. Each marriage is different and every couple has their own set of boundaries and expectations. The word of God is to be the foundation of all boundaries observed by husband and wife. If the couple operates within the boundaries personally established and supported by God, then the marriage will experience great pleasure and fulfillment.

> " [1]*And it shall come to pass, if thou shalt hearken diligently unto the voice of the LORD thy God, to observe and to do all his commandments which I command thee this day, that the LORD thy God will set thee on high above all nations of the earth:* [2]*And all these blessings shall come on thee, and overtake thee, if thou shalt hearken unto the voice of the LORD thy God."*
> Deuteronomy 28:1-2

Blessing falls on your house when you operate within the boundaries God has set, which is simply abiding by His word. When you are at work, you are blessed and when you are lounging around the house in a t-shirt and shorts you are blessed. Your children, they too, like everything else, are blessed. Everything you own or can dream of owning is blessed. No opponent can ever triumph over you and nothing you do can fail. Everywhere you go, the blessing of the Lord follows. This is because of the rule associated with the boundary God has established. The rule says that if you observe the commands of the Lord you will be blessed.

When you observe the boundaries set in your marriage, you experience each others best. He is in a great mood when he comes home. He has called and texted you all day. He can't wait to arrive to massage your feet and to hear all about your day. And you are just as excited to see him as well. You can't wait to draw a bath for the two of you, after sharing his favorite dinner. Both husband and wife enjoy participated in expressing acts of love. They desire to pray together, study the word together, to share everything they enjoy doing individually, together.

If the bounds God set are ignored, division, disappointment, and disaster occur.

> " [15]*But it shall come to pass, if thou wilt not hearken unto the voice of the LORD thy God, to observe to do all his commandments and his statutes which I command thee this day; that all these curses shall come upon thee, and overtake thee:*"
> Deuteronomy 28:15

You now find yourself frustrated at work. Everything about the job stinks. To make matters worse, the wages aren't close to being enough to cover expenses. Everywhere you go it seems like a rain cloud follows and rains down disappointment.

Curses also fall on your marriage when boundaries are ignored. Both spouses dread coming home. They both work as late as possible and make as may stops as they can on the way home. There is no enticing aroma coming from the kitchen, only one of stinky garbage since the bag hasn't been emptied all week. The two barely speak and they spend as much time on opposite sides of the house. Discord, unresolved issues and wounded feelings result when boundaries are ignored or overstepped.

Like many books in the Bible, in the book of Judges, we see a birth, a promise, a purpose, and a boundary. Manoah and his wife were unable to bear children. One day, Manoah's wife was approached by an angel. She was informed that the Lord would bless her with a child that she previously was unable to conceive.

> "[3] *The angel of the LORD appeared to her and said, "You are sterile and childless, but you are going to conceive and have a son.* [4] *Now see to it that you drink no wine or other fermented drink and that you do not eat anything unclean,* [5] *because you will conceive and give birth to a son. No razor may be used on his head, because the boy is to be a Nazirite, set apart to God from birth, and he will begin the deliverance of Israel from the hands of the Philistines."*

Judges 13:3-5 NIV

God is able to make the humanly impossible, possible. He sends a word to the couple and presents a promise followed by instruction. The woman is to not drink wine or to eat anything impure. After the child is born, she was to never cut his hair because he is dedicated to the Lord. The birth we see for Monoah's wife involves the revitalization of her womb. She is promised a son, and his purpose is to begin the deliverance of a nation. The boundary stipulates that she must not consume anything that will be detrimental to the child; she is also never to cut his hair. The woman did as God commanded. As a result she reaped the benefits of the birth, promise, purpose and boundary. She gave birth to a son and his life was blessed as he grew from a young boy into a man.

When God brings a husband and wife together, He births a new thing to fulfill a purpose. A household that seeks God and follows His precepts are promised a life of abundance. The essential element is that they must obey the voice of the Lord, adhering to his boundaries. A couple that is obedient reaps the benefits of the blessing.

Samson grows and begins to live out the purpose of the Lord. He possesses great strength and has the ability to overcome the Philistines. His strength is attached to the boundary set by God. He was never to cut his hair because that was the God given source of his strength. However, there came a time when his boundaries were tested.

After Samson's first wife was killed by the Philistines, Samson fell in love with another Philistine woman, Delilah. The Philistine leaders became aware of Samson's affections for Delilah and decided to use her as a means to defeat Samson. They approached Delilah with a proposition. In exchange for silver, she was to uncover the source of Samson insurmountable strength. So Delilah asked Samson to tell her the source of his strength so that he may be tied and afflicted.

Delilah did not truly care about Samson's boundaries because she choose to act upon her own selfish desires. Delilah had malice intentions and false motives. She chose to be cunning and use her attractive nature to lure Samson out of bounds and away from his purpose. However, Samson did not succumb to her seductions. Instead he gave her a false story to gratify her season of questioning. Delilah then repeated what Samson told her to the Philistines. And when they came to attack him, Samson was able to break free from being bound, and defeat them every time.

Violation of a boundary always involves false motives. What gives a partner strength and definition of character are boundaries. But sometimes those boundaries don't work for the other person. It's not that they are unreasonable or in violation of another person's boundaries; someone just wants to be in control. One spouse wishes to bind the other spouse so that they can conquer them in a particular area. God given boundaries are not to be removed, waived, or ignored. They are not up for negotiation.

In tennis, if the ball is served out of bounds two consecutive times, the other team receives a point. This is because a defined boundary line was drawn. The rule say there is leeway on the first serve but consequence after the second. Though the boundaries are set, an official has to enforce the rules. There is no arguing or debating. The rules are the rules, and the ball went out of bounds.

Because Samson did not immediately enforce the rules to his boundary, Delilah was allowed to enter a series of negotiations with Samson.

> *" 15And she said unto him, How canst thou say, I love thee, when thine heart is not with me? thou hast mocked me these three times, and hast not told me wherein thy great strength lieth. 16And it came to pass, when she pressed him daily with her words, and urged him, so that his soul was vexed unto death; 17That he told her all his heart, and said unto her, There hath not come a razor upon mine head; for I have been a Nazarite unto God from my mother's womb: if I be shaven, then my strength will go from me, and I shall become weak, and be like any other man."*
> Judges 16:15-17

With time, the line that clearly marked a boundary became warn. Eventually it was no longer observed.

Love is a very powerful force. When a man loves a woman, there isn't anything he wouldn't do for her. When a woman loves a man, she will stop at nothing to please him. One can not forget that love means operating within the other person's boundaries.

We love God first. Because we love Him, we do as He commands. We live a life pleasing to Him and worship

Him with all that we have. The marital relationship is a gift from God. It is to be used to worship Him and to fulfill His purpose. When one tries to alter the boundaries of their spouse, one is pulling the other away from their purpose.

After Samson tells Delilah where his strength lies, she uses the information against him. The Philistines bring her silver in exchange for their enemy, Samson. Delilah lulls Samson to sleep and cuts off the source of his strength. When the Philistines come to attack Samson he is overcome and taken captive. His eyes are gouged and he is forced to work in prison. Delilah benefited while Samson suffered. In the end, God restored Samson and he was able to bring down a temple and kill many of his enemies. But Samson also lost his life in the process.

Lack of observing boundaries can bring ruin to a relationship. A husband may not become the man he is to be because his wife uses the power of manipulation and suggestion to get what she desires. For silver, a new house, a luxury car, she may press her spouse with words until he gives in. The finances they were to use to start a business were used for other reasons. Now the husband resents his wife because they are not in the place that was to produce his occupational fulfillment and provide financial subsistence. He had a boundary set by God that was not observed. A wife abandons a vision because of her husband's insecurities. She pretends not to be intelligent or to have an opinion. He curses her and belittles her to fortify an ego. She intern withdraws from everyone and misses out on touching all the lives she would have by fulfilling her God given assignment.

The word of God is the first and final authority. It establishes our boundaries as believers. It is important to remember that we are accountable to God for our actions. If He has brought a man and a woman together it is to birth something from them together. They have to stay in bounds to fulfill his purpose. Samson was able to kill more Philistines at the end of his life than he did in the beginning. How much more could he have accomplished if he would have stayed in bounds throughout the entire course?

Evaluate your life. Do you have clearly defined boundaries, supported by God's word? Are those boundaries immovable? Or are you pressing someone to remove their boundaries for self gain? The word of God says,

"*17 Cursed is the man who moves his neighbor's boundary stone.*"
Deuteronomy 27:13 NIV

What may seem to be of benefit today, will surly bring misfortune tomorrow. A triangle isn't supposed to be a square and a square was not designed to be a triangle. The lines that connect them, support them, and define them are to be immovable. Know who you are in Christ, understand your spouse's importance to the kingdom, shape your lives the way there were designed, and always remember to stay in bounds.

chapter 10

Speak On It

"Honey, why do you do that," she gripes in frustration?

"Do what," he responds cluelessly?

"What you just did? It really bothers me."

"Oh! I never knew that. You never told me."

"Oh but I did, a million times," she thought as she rolled her eyes and walked away.

Communication is an important part of marriage. Your spouse can't read you mind nor can you read his. The only way to understand one another's desires is through communication with God and each other.

Do you remember stories from your mothers or grandmothers that entailed Sunday afternoons of sharing while preparing a large meal for the family? These times involved the dissemination of knowledge from old to young, sister to sister, friend to friend. The opportunity to follow the instructions found in the book of Titus were seized.

> *"³Likewise, teach the older women to be reverent in the way they live, not to be slanderers or addicted to much wine, but to teach what is good. ⁴Then they can train the younger women to love their husbands and children, ⁵to be self-controlled and pure, to be busy at home, to be kind, and to be subject to their husbands, so that no one will malign the word of God."*
> Titus 2:3-5 NIV

It seems now that as families are spread apart and close friends are hard to find, sharing of stories and experiences have faded. We may on occasion get to hear something useful at work or during an after hours function, but most of that information is garbage. *"Girl if I were you!" "And girl did you see him!"* We hear nothing but the best advice from those who are operating off the worst principles. Second Timothy 2:16 says,

> *"Avoid godless chatter, because those who indulge in it will become more and more ungodly."* NIV

Gossip is like a black hole that swallows your time and energy and leaves you with nothing but emptiness. You didn't gain knowledge, only foolish words, that if applied to your life will produce a foolish outcome. Psalms1:1 says,

"¹Blessed is the man that walketh not in the counsel of the ungodly, nor standeth in the way of sinners, nor sitteth in the seat of the scornful."

The purpose of conversation is to receive or provide information on a particular issue. However, the word of God says you won't find your blessing in conversation with the wicked. Yes, some of your friends may be wicked. It's that person who dresses in a devil costume every year for Halloween. You love them like Christ commands and you pray that the Lord saves them, but know that wisdom is found in Godly advice. Those who pursue God passionately are those you should surround yourselves with. If the fruit in your life isn't sweet, it may be because you have a contaminated stream watering your fertile ground.

When you begin to surround yourself with godly women, you will notice the topics of conversation will change. Not only will you feel uplifted, you will find that you are able to discuss principles that actually work. If you have been married or dating for some time, have you noticed that there are things that are different from when you first met your significant other? Maybe the romance isn't the happily ever after you expected. Possibly the allocation and distribution of resources seems to come more from your way than originally planned, and there is very little help around the house to balance the load. It could be that you are not getting the attention that you need. Are you competing with the sports channels, video games, hobbies with the guys? Is there time for everything else but you? Whatever your issues are, you should SPEAK ON IT!

At some point you should communicate to your spouse in a *__gentle__* manner how you feel. God tells us to,

> "[19]*Wherefore, my beloved brethren, let every man be swift to hear, slow to speak, slow to wrath.*"
> James 1:19

Observing the stop sign before allowing words to leave your lips, provides a moment to curtail them and avoid having a head on collision. It is also possible, however, that no matter how gentle your words are, they will not be well received. In either event, repeating yourself a million times isn't going to magically change the situation. Keeping silent isn't going get the job done either. What you should do is pray.

"Yeah, yeah, I've heard that before."

No...really, pray. Matthew 7: 7 says,

> "[7]*Ask, and it shall be given you; seek, and ye shall find; knock, and it shall be opened unto you.*"

Ask God to show you if you are doing anything that is inhibiting the result you seek.

> *"How can you say to your brother, 'Brother, let me take the speck out of your eye,' when you yourself fail to see the plank in your own eye? You hypocrite, first take the plank out of*

your eye, and then you will see clearly to remove the speck from your brother's eye" Luke 6:42 NIV

At times it is easier to clearly observe what the other person has done wrong or can improve upon. We fail to think that we have done anything remotely to contribute to the situation. Take a step back and closely evaluate your words, actions or lack thereof. A change in attitude may solicit an alternative response. Save the heart to heart conversation for issues that impact the relationship. You may have had so many sit downs with your spouse that his rear is raw. He zones out before you even begin to speak. Table minor things like the toilet seat that was left up or the pair of shoes that have been by the door for a few days. Those items may be better received by changing the way they are packaged and delivered.

After you have initiated the process of change by starting with self, ask God for what you would like to see different in your relationship from your spouse. Words are power activated by faith. Everyday, start speaking on your spouse. "Today he will come home straight from work." Watch how his buddies one by one cancel on him. "Today he will spend time with me." Watch as the power goes off and he can't watch television or play video games. "Today he will be motivated to follow a dream." Observe how he starts to plan for his business or apply for a new job. Sometimes when we discuss with our mate how we feel, they are not in a position to receive what we are saying. They may be distracted by outside influences, internal feelings of inadequacy, or lack the connection with

God. Know that even if our spouses can not hear you at the time, God can. He alone has the power to change any and everything. He can open any blind eye and every closed door. Your words bring life and have the power to produce. Speak on it, believe, relax, and see it!

Words are not only important when it comes to communicating thoughts and soliciting change, they are important in our daily walk with Christ. Whatever your flavor, Passion Red, Strawberry Kiwi, or Medicated Balm for that supper chapped day, we take time to dress our lips in sexy glosses and colors to plump them up and to accentuate their beauty. Some days we even line them for that extra POP. It's amazing how diligent we are with making our lips attractive to the eye, but not to the ear. Like gloss that wears throughout the day, so are the sweet words that flow from our mouths. All it takes is for a co-worker to make you mad and you go from Dr. Jekyll to Mrs. Hyde, ready to tear down everyone and everything in your path with your words. A 5 '3", 120 pound woman can bring down the house, literally, with the tiny, sweetly glossed mouth.

Words have a strong impact, more than one may realize. With them we can build and also destroy. Just know that whatever dwelling you construct, you are going to have to live in. Proverbs 13: 2—3 tells us,

"²*A man shall eat good by the fruit of his mouth: but the soul of the transgressors shall eat violence.* ³*He that keepeth* *his mouth keepeth his life: but he that openeth wide his lips shall have destruction."*

Why is it that people don't seem to come around or stay around often? Could it be that your words have built you a shack, one with shoddy floor boards and paper-thin walls? There is little appeal for anyone to come and see what the place has to offer. They question if you are unreliable, like the weak floors board, or if the time of sharing will seep through your paper-thin lips to someone else.

Have you ever heard of the saying, "you are going to eat your words?" It's true. You will. Proverbs 18:21 says,

"[21]Death and life are in the power of the tongue: and they that love it shall eat the fruit."

When you get angry and decide to curse your spouse, your boss or the girl that looked at you funny, you are cursing your fruit. Even if you do not curse them to their faces, the result is the same. Maybe your husband was going to take you out to dinner tonight at your favorite restaurant. He may have been late because he was at the jewelry store picking up something nice for you. Those are the things you prayed for, right? You cursed your blessing. What about the promotion and raise you so deserve? Remember blessings and promotions come from God not from the company written at the top of you pay check. Why bother cursing your boss when he or she doesn't control your progress anyway? The girl that looked at you cross-eyed probably saw Jesus on you and was wondering how she could get him too.

James 3:9—12 says,

"[9]With *the tongue we praise our Lord and Father, and with it we curse men, who have been made in God's likeness.* [10]*Out of the same mouth come praise and cursing. My brothers, this should not be.* [11]*Can both fresh water and salt[a] water flow from the same spring?* [12]*My brothers, can a fig tree bear olives, or a grapevine bear figs? Neither can a salt spring produce fresh water.*" NIV

Good words and bad words should not come from the same mouth. The people in our lives are God's children too. They are our parents, spouses, sisters, brothers, friends, and even strangers. No matter who they are, or what small or large offense committed, we can not curse them with the same tongue we praise God with. Though the world may not agree, it is best to be fat from the utterance of positive words than impoverished by speaking negative ones. If you want to eat well from the fruit of your lips, speak positive words that align with the word of God. We have what we say!

As you go throughout the day and freshen your lip wear, remember to say something positive about your spouse, your job, your situation. As good as your lips look when you close that little compact, so too will be the results in your life.

chapter 11

Plan B

GOD IS THE Alpha and Omega, the first and the last, beginning and end. There is nothing before him and nothing that follows. God needs no contingency. The work of His hands never fails.

> "9 *Remember the former things, those of long ago; I am God, and there is no other; I am God, and there is none like me.* 10 *I make known the end from the beginning, from ancient times, what is still to come. I say: My purpose will stand, and I will do all that I please."*
> Isaiah 46:9-10 NIV

Wherever God brought you from or is bringing you through, His plan is in action. It was designed well before your existence and executed with His word. Think about it. If God doesn't need a plan B, why do we? Why do we have a backup for something that isn't designed to fail? Even if we've been praying and speaking on the issues of our hearts, do we believe that God will answer our prayers? It boils down to a trust issue. Proverbs 3: 5-6 says,

"⁵Trust in the LORD with all thine heart; and lean not unto thine own understanding. ⁶In all thy ways acknowledge him, and he shall direct thy paths."

When we don't understand the things that are transpiring in our lives, we begin to strategize. If I move this here, then this will happen. If I take some from there, that will occur. Our own wit and knowledge is relied upon and applied to a situation in effort to produce a desired result. Pressure isn't always needed to bring about change. There are instances when change comes with time.

Have you ever tried to hurry along the cooking process? You turned up the heat as high as it could go. Before long, the outside appeared to be done, nice and golden; but when you bit down, the inside remained raw. This resulted because the cooking process was not allowed to complete its course, in its designated timing. Externally the food appeared to be done, but internally, the process was not yet complete. Sometimes we rush into things. We may act in ill-advised ways to obtain wealth or status quickly. We may start a venture without having all the important details, or we may procure a relationship prematurely. We do whatever it takes to get what we want, when we want it, irrespective of God's timing. Sometimes, however, we aren't always ready to handle the abundance associated with the object of our desires. On the outside we look ready, but the inside is spiritually undercooked and slightly raw. So what happens? More often times than not, the wealth alludes us, the business does not perform as expected, and the relationship has holes in it. The success hoped for is met with disappointment because we moved out of season.

Stages in life are analogous to seasons. Winter doesn't come before fall nor does summer before spring.

"¹To every thing there is a season, and a time to every purpose under the heaven."
Ecclesiastes 3:1

If seasons did not follow sequential order, how would one prepare for life? Would you walk around in the summer sun with rain boots and umbrella? Would you attempt to lay out in the snow in shorts and a tank top? You certainly could, but some behavior is best suited for the appropriate season. You may prefer one to the other, all but are required. The season that you are currently in but don't really care for, will at some point change.

Imagine the first signs of spring when the flowers begin to bloom. But then the last frost of winter comes and kills the first signs of spring. We don't become dismayed that the first sign of our change has been delayed because we know that spring is going to come. The same is true with breakthrough. When we are in a season of testing and it appears that finally the change has come, we should not be discouraged and begin to prepare for winter to last all year. If God made you a promise and gave a word that He will deliver you and change your situation, He will. A season is just that, a season. It can not last always.

Present purpose is associated with current time. You can't watch a program in Pacific Standard Time if you live on the east coast. There is a scheduled program for where you are, right here, right now. Once the broadcast concludes, the program is over. There are no highlights or reruns. That means you can't war with your spouse forever over the same issues. There were no highlights to the fight. You discuss the issues, pray over them, and move on with the answer God gives. Your spouse may have done something hurtful that tore down your wall of trust. You go through the season of crying, being distant not speaking, and possibly being angry. That season is overshadowed and replaced with a season of mending, rebuilding, loving, embracing, and laughing.

It is not human intellect but the wisdom and encouragement of God that brings us through those difficult seasons. God knows everything, the past, present, and future. What you are planning may not work. Though it was intended for good, it could turn out terribly. Holding on to a plan B and the little black book is a strong indicator that you don't completely trust in the Lord's capability to oversee every season in your life.

Difficulty by definition is associated with complexity, those things that are complicated, something that isn't easy. A present challenge doesn't indicate that God has abandoned you and that you should take matters into your own hands. Difficulty presents an opportunity for growth. The Bible says in James 1:2-4,

"*²My brethren, count it all joy when ye fall into divers temptations; ³Knowing this, that the trying of your faith worketh patience. ⁴But let patience have her perfect work, that ye may be perfect and entire, wanting nothing.*"

How can you be joyous when experiencing difficulty? There is nothing warm and fuzzy about hard times. Joy comes from understanding that the temporal things are developing us. It is a period of refining. When a clay pot is put into a fiery kiln, it comes out smooth, lustrous, and beautiful. It isn't as clumpy or as rough as it was before it went in. We are similar to the pot in the kiln. The fire might be intense, but when we come out, we will be better than we were before we went in. Rest knowing that God is aware of every decision and move we will make. Whether the ride is along his path or our own, He is with us.

When a child learns to ride a bicycle they start with training wheels. They learn how to balance their weight on the bike so that it doesn't lean too much to the right or to the left. The training wheels are there so that if they do tilt, the wheels will continue to roll and the child will not fall. But eventually, the child outgrows training wheels and must ride without them. Prior exposure developed the skills needed to ride without trainers.

The first time cycling without the extra wheels may be a tad intimidating, but mom or dad is holding onto the back of the seat and walking alongside to make sure their child doesn't fall. Faster the pedaling feet go and now mom or dad is running to keep up. Their child hasn't fallen yet. They haven't leaned too much to the right or overpowered the left. The training before taught them to be well balanced. Eventually the parent lets go and the child doesn't realize that he or she are riding all by themselves as their parents watch with a sense of pride and joy.

Trials in life are periods where we have training wheels on. We learn how to ride up and down hills, through puddles, and on curbs without falling. Then the next phase of life comes and once again God is there holding on to us so that we don't fall. If for a moment we do take our eyes off of Him and begin to wobble, He has the back of or seat and can stabilize us.

God knows that He has equipped us with the skills we need to ride throughout life and not fall. He empowers, entrusts, and enjoys watching us ride through the seasons. Though we may not feel Him right behind us, He never leaves. Year after year we grow. We move from a six speed bike to a ten speed. With each transition, we become better riders.

Plan B's are shortcuts through progression.

"I don't want to go through all of that to become better."

"I don't like where I am right now, so I am going someplace else."

What you see and have is relative to where you are. Cutting progression short is cutting God short. There is a saying that goes, "the grass isn't always greener on the other side." Another is, "all that glitters is not gold." Though something may be appeasing to the eye it may not in reality be as it appears. What you have may actually be better. Getting caught up in appearances may cause you to pursue a plan B outside the will of the Father.

God instructs us not to desire what someone else has. We are not to want another person's house, husband, car, job or anything that doesn't have your name on it. If it is suppose to be your house, your name will appear on the deed. If the car belongs to you, the registration will be in your name. If the man lying next to you is truly yours, both his name and yours will appear on a marriage license. Anything God wants you to have, He will give you the title to.

Emotions or lack of control thereof, causes individuals to claim what they are not entitled to. The emotions that typically steer a person to plan B are anger, envy, fear, disappointment, and distrust.

"My husband makes me so mad; I could spit fire. He doesn't make time for me or appreciate me."

Because of your anger you begin to fantasize about what you desire; not with your husband but with someone else.

"I wish I had a man that would..."

The thoughts lead you to consider an alternative to the present situation. Plan Alpha that God gave you is no longer good enough. Your Plan B sounds better. If anger and envy go unchecked, they can lead you into adultery or some other area outside the will of God.

> *[1]What causes fights and quarrels among you? Don't they come from your desires that battle within you? [2]You want something but don't get it. You kill and covet, but you cannot have what you want. You quarrel and fight. You do not have, because you do not ask God. [3]When you ask, you do not receive, because you ask with wrong motives, that you may spend what you get on your pleasures."*
> James 4:1-3 NIV

An unmet desire may be the result of ulterior motive. Fights and constant bickering stem from a coveting heart, one willing to manipulate and do anything to get what it wants. The Lord seeks to grant the desires of our heart. He doesn't block our attempts to be happy. Any issue, including marital, God can resolve. If we ask for help, He will provide it as long as it is not contradict who He is. God alone has the power to change a person. But He has to be invited into the relationship to improve any underperforming area.

When a major corporation is experiencing financial difficulty, instead of closing shop at the first sign of trouble, they will commonly call in a consultant that specializes in financial revitalization. It is the consultant's responsibility to objectively evaluate any underperform-ing areas that are a hindrance to the company's growth. Once those areas are identified, the consultant puts to-gether a plan of action that entails a restructuring of op-erations. Over a period of time, the company moves away from poorly performing operations and embarks upon those that are beneficial to the organization as a whole. When we invite Christ into our hearts, He becomes our consultant. He cares compassionately about the tiniest of concerns and seeks to improve the areas where we strug-gle. Rev 3:20 says,

*"**[20]Behold, I stand at the door, and knock: if any man hear my voice, and open the door, I will come in to him, and will sup with him, and he with me."*

The Lord is calling you and waiting for you to let Him in, not only for eternal salvation but also for current deliverance. What good is having the omnipotent advisor on your team if you make Him sit in the reception area? You have access to the greatest resource but don't employ Him.

God alone has the master plan. Though your best ef-forts were given, the plan without God's input won't turn things around. Your own resources, intelligence, and en-ergy will eventually be exhausted.

Open up your life completely; show God the books, company trademarks and secrets. He knows them any-way. Grant God direct access, yield to His will and allow

Him to take complete control of your situation. Over a period of days, months, years, you will see Him take you from glory to glory. Your third and forth quarter will no longer be in the slumps. The board meetings with the family will be celebratory. Your life will turn around in such a way that the only plan you will ever need and trust is the one of the Almighty God.

chapter 12

Not the End of the World

As YOU CONTINUE to grow, walk with God and trust Him, you will begin to see that there isn't anything He can't handle. People say all of the time, "nothing is too hard for God." They say it so much that it is often regarded as cliché. The impact of His power is reduced to mere words without the application of faith. Truly nothing is outside of His authority or too hard for Him. There is no situation that He can not fix or time when He isn't in control.

You may not be in a present state of knowing what is going on in your life. You may feel powerless and lack ability to control or influence your situation. You may have taken such a blow that your vision is temporally blurred and hearing impaired. You can't see straight or discern the voice of the Lord. In moments where we feel lost, confused, isolated, or distressed, God picks us up and carriers us. He carries us until we find our strength in Him to walk again. Second Corinthians 12:19 reassures us that the grace of God is more than enough and He fortifies every weak area with His strength. In those cumbersome hours and overwhelming moments of weakness, God is the power we need to pull through.

The first thing that we need to remember when our faith is being tested is that it is not the end of the world. After the great flood in Genesis, God said,

"And never again will I destroy all living creatures, as I have done"
Genesis 8:21 NIV

If you haven't heard the sounding of trumpets signifying our saviors' return, your mortal life is not over. There is much left for you to do. I say this in all seriousness. When difficulties face us, sometimes we feel as if our lives can't or won't go on. It will. We usually don't plan for a natural disaster, for a twister, earthquake, or flood. The damage and losses sustained were unanticipated. But those affected by the disaster recover. God will restore you to a condition that is better than before.

In Genesis, after man was created, God commanded man not to eat from the tree of the knowledge of good and evil. One day, the serpent appeared to Eve and tricked her into eating from the tree God said not to eat from. Because of man's disobedience to God, sin entered the earth and man was cursed. Women now experience pain in childbirth and men work to provide for their families. There became a separation from God, the life man would live, greatly differed from the life man was called to live.

Genesis shows us the fall of man and 2 Timothy reveals his restoration. God sent his only son Jesus to die for us and to restore our quality of life here on earth and eternally with Him. He went through the process of saving our souls, forgiving us of our sin, and restoring us to our rightful place, will He not restore any broken area of our lives?

There are many things that try to wrinkle the fabric of our character and moths that come to eat wholes into what covers us. Daily wrinkles, though annoying, can be easily ironed out and pesky bugs exterminated. It is those big trails that take all that is in us to stand. Psalms 23:4 says,

> "⁴*Yea, though I walk through the valley of the shadow of death, I will fear no evil: for thou art with me; thy rod and thy staff they comfort me.*"

Sometimes there are valleys so deep in our lives we feel as if we will die. We curl up in a tight ball in the shower or in the closet and weep without secession. We cry aloud until our voice has faded and tears can't fall any more. And when there is no energy left in our bodies to wail any longer, we fall asleep feeling helpless and alone.

When we walk through the lowest valleys, the word of God says that we are not to be afraid because God is with us. This is the first point to note: no matter the situation, God is with you.

The enemy's job is to try to destroy you. You are on a battle field and the war rages within your mind. However, you are a mighty woman of God, put here on earth for a specific purpose. No one else can fulfill the purpose God called you to fill, but you. Though there is one body in Christ, there are many parts to the body. You are needed for your part.

When you are going through difficulty, the deceiver will portray that you are all alone. If he can get you to buy into the idea that you don't have a support system, then you will start to believe that you can't survive. Your words will start to be words of doubt and actions will lack faith. Your valley will truly become a deeper pit, or you will become lost in the abyss, because you took your eyes off of Jesus. When Peter walked on water in Matthew 14:30, he began to sink because he got distracted by the rough wind and crashing waves. He took his eyes off of the Lord.

"30But when he saw the wind boisterous, he was afraid; and beginning to sink, he cried, saying, Lord, save me."

The storm and the wind were so great that he feared. This leads to point number two. Do not fear; focus on the Lord. Keep your eyes fixed on Him. When tragic events occur, a fear sets in that the event will happen again. We think nothing or no one can protect us from feeling the pain again. We find ourselves in a valley accompanied by reluctance, fear, and doubt. Sometimes we stay in the valley because we are in a state of self pity. Self pity is a pit dug by ourselves for ourselves. Our heads are hung low. We can't believe this has happened to us. We didn't do anything to deserve being lied to, mislead, abused, or cheated on.

We throw a huge celebration in honor of our pity. And once the party is over, if it every ends, we refuse to leave. We wallow in our woes forever. We don't allow others to love us or comfort us, even God. That really stinks. Who wants to be miserable forever? The third thing you should do is allow God to comfort you.

It doesn't feel good to be hurt or disappointed. It's nice to loose weight but not because food doesn't taste good anymore and you can't eat or sleep. You spend all day throwing up because your stomach is unsettled and all night crying and dreaming of an end. Know this, dismay can't last all day. Psalms 30:5 says,

> "*Weeping may endure for a night, But joy comes in the morning.*" NIV

What this means is that you don't need a month's supply of tissue or eye drops. Your weeping, pain, and discomfort are only for a short moment. Psst...a mere passing of gas in the wind. It stinks for a while but then it's gone. Life is to be a celebration of redemption. Jesus is our savior, deliverer, and comforter. Fix your eyes on

Him, lean on Him; let Him wrap you up in His goodness and the comfort of His word. Isaiah 54: 4—6 says,

> [4] *"Do not be afraid; you will not suffer shame. Do not fear disgrace; you will not be humiliated. You will forget the shame of your youth and remember no more the reproach of your widowhood. [5] For your Maker is your husband—the LORD Almighty is his name—the Holy One of Israel is your Redeemer; he is called the God of all the earth. [6] The LORD will call you back as if you were a wife deserted and distressed in spirit—a wife who married young, only to be rejected,"* says your God." NIV

Once again we see that we are not to fear. What transpired will not be like a scarlet letter to your name. You don't have to feel embarrassed or ashamed. Forget what has been. The party is over. It doesn't exist any longer. If your point of pain is from something you have done, God forgives all sins and forgets them the moment you ask him to. You should do the same. The only person holding you to your mistake is you.

If someone else wounded your heart deeply, allow God to restore you as He is our redeemer. Even if the pain was caused by someone close to you, your mother, father, uncle, cousin, or husband. God fills the void. He is like your husband in unity with you. He will call you back from the place of disappointment and distress. Point number four, is to call on God.

When Peter began to sink, he cried out to Jesus, "Lord, save me!" After he cried out, Jesus retrieved him from the vast ocean that sought to swallow him. Psalms 91:15 says,

"¹⁵He shall call upon me, and I will answer him: I will be with him in trouble; I will deliver him, and honour him."

Since we are not operating in a state of fear, call on God; He will rescue you. You are crying and screaming, and yelling anyway. Your nose is running a marathon, tissues are scattered everywhere, and you look distressed. The Girlfriend Go Get Him Squad, nor mom or dad can come to your rescue. No one is with you at every moment but Jesus. He is the only one that can hear you and simultaneously help you.

Stop rehearsing the problem and the pain, and call on Him for help. God is available 24/7. When no one is awake at 2:00 A.M. and you need someone to talk to, call on God. If no one else responds to you because it's the weekend, call on God. He doesn't go on vacation, isn't off for the holidays, nor does He close His doors due to bad weather.

When a storm is brewing in your life, call on God! He has the emergency response you need. Tell him what you want, expect Him to grant your request, and wait until your life raft of miracles and deliverance show up. A person stranded on a raft in the ocean does not decide after an hour of waiting that they are going to jump into the water and drown or be devoured by sharks because the rescue team has not arrived. They wait with great expectation that they will be rescued soon. Hebrews 6:12

tells us we must simply implore faith and patience to receive. God will answer your requests if you simply call upon him.

It can be difficult during seasons of recovery to wait on the Lord. Feelings of anger and unforgiveness creep in and seek to take root. Those feelings are like weeds in a beautiful garden. We can't enjoy the roses because of the crab grass. Remember in the Garden of Eden, the serpent seduced Eve into believing she had to taste fruit from the only forbidden tree. Momentarily, she forgot about all the other trees she had to enjoy and eat from. Sometimes we forget about all the good things around us and only focus on the bad. The more we focus on the negative, the angrier and bitterer we become, allowing sin to ensue.

The Bible says,

"In your anger do not sin;"
Psalms 4:4 NIV

"Dearly beloved, avenge not yourselves, but rather give place unto wrath: for it is written, Vengeance is mine; I will repay, saith the Lord,"
Romans 12:19

God can handle a situation better than you can. You don't have to call the woman who committed adultery with your husband and curse her. You don't need to slash any tires or send your brother to beat anybody up. We understand the principles of seed and harvest. Whatever a person sews, that person will receive the consequences of that seed. Is it really worth ending up in jail or missing out on the blessing that God has for you because you took matters into your own hands? The adulteress will have to answer to God, as will your spouse, as will you. The Bible says,

"37Judge not, and ye shall not be judged: condemn not, and ye shall not be condemned: forgive, and ye shall be forgiven:" Luke 6:37

Everyone makes mistakes, okay, maybe not that particular mistake but we are not in a position to judge. We can't tell him and her to go straight to Hades and burn forever. We are to operate in forgiveness. It is important to forgive no matter the offense.

In Matthew 18:21-22 Peter asks Jesus a question,

"21Then came Peter to him, and said, Lord, how oft shall my brother sin against me, and I forgive him? till seven times? 22Jesus saith unto him, I say not unto thee, Until seven times: but, Until seventy times seven."

This doesn't mean that you should start counting. It means that when someone sins against you and they sincerely ask for forgiveness, you should forgive them. Forgiveness is not for the other person, forgiveness is for you. A lack of forgiveness will hold you in the past or present and prevent you from moving into your future. It may cause you to separate yourself from God as you yourself begin to operate in sin. You may even do to your offender the same thing that they did to you.

Lack of forgiveness produces lack of wholeness. So irrespective of the offender's posture, it is important to operate in forgiveness. Forgiveness removes you from bondage of the memory and brings you closer to the calling of Christ.

The last step to recovery is to rest in the promise. God's words to us are guarantees. Because He can not lie, everything He says is a promise. What He said has to happen. In Isaiah 61, the spirit of broken heartedness is bound and those who are held captive by their past or pain are set free. The Lord's favor rests upon you and He avenges and comforts those who are saddened. Isaiah 61:3-4, 7 continues by saying God will,

> *"give unto them beauty for ashes, the oil of joy for mourning, the garment of praise for the spirit of heaviness; that they might be called trees of righteousness, the planting of the LORD, that he might be glorified. [4]And they shall build the old wastes, they shall raise up the former desolations, and they shall repair the waste cities, the desolations of many generations. [7]For your shame ye shall have double; and for confusion they shall rejoice in their portion: therefore in their land they shall possess the double: everlasting joy shall be unto them."* NIV

Rest assured that God will comfort and avenge. The hurt and confusion you currently feel is only temporary and you will have overflowing, everlasting joy. The downtrodden faced, weak frame, crumbled sprit will be made beautiful again. There will be no more heaviness from the shambles of your life. You will be rebuilt and restored.

God will not only restore you, He will multiply you for all of your agony. You'll be in better shape than you were before the storm. Whatever you are going through, know that nothing is too hard for God. The storm can not last. The waters will recede. The wind will stop blowing, and the valley will turn into a mountain top. It is not the end of the world, but an opportunity for God to change your world into something new.

chapter 13

<u>Ever After</u>

SPEECHLESS, NUMB, A state of disbelief, you shake your head trying and awake from the trance. There is an overwhelming sense of joy that can't be articulated to the smallest degree. You've entering into a surreal state of rest, no longer in arms reach but now clenched tightly. A sense of triumph and gratitude surrounds you. You prayed fervently, believed earnestly, endured patiently, and have now overcome every obstacle in your life with God directing every victory. Your life is like a fairytale with Jesus as the orator.

Have you ever wondered why all the fairytales end the same way? The guy gets the girl, they ride off into the sunset and the words, *"Happily Ever After."* appear. The meaning of the phrase is usually taken at face value, and little to no thought is given to what the ever after entails. We simply trust the couple will be happy forever, even beyond death, for all eternity. Rarely do we wonder how they are doing, are they still together, has the kingdom been overtaken by calamity. We don't question something we already have the answer to. The details vary but every story is structured the same. A background is established followed by a conflict, a turning point is reached, the conflict is resolved and there is a happy ending. The punctuation to, "Happily Ever After" is important. A period ends the sentence not ellipses. There is nothing to follow the happy ending, no more conflict or need for resolution.

As children, we believe that anything is possible. We believe in fairytales and happy endings. No dragon is too fierce to face or too hard to slay. We dream big and anticipate hope meeting expectation. As we age, dreams are deferred and hope fades. The faith we had in a "happily ever after" is almost non existent. Proverbs 13:12 says,

" [12]*Hope deferred maketh the heart sick: but when the desire cometh, it is a tree of life.*"

Having hope is vital because it breaths life to our souls. Hope erodes disappointment, eliminates fear, and conquers depression. Hope encompasses our aspirations, desires, dreams, and visions. The Bible says in Proverbs 29:18 that people die when they lack vision.

There has to be something to look forward to, to strive toward. If there is nothing waiting in the days ahead, it makes it difficult to push forward.

"My grandmother was alone, my mom was alone, and I suspect I will be alone."

"Julia died of cancer, Aunt Wilma died of cancer, and I will probably die the same way."

Anticipating a generational curse to fall on you is a form of perverted hope. Your heart is sick because the vision of the future is bleak. It is possible to find yourself in the place that you expected because faith is the activator of hope. The build up of hope's kinetic energy is released when faith is applied. Hebrews 11:1 tell us,

"[1]Now faith is the substance of things hoped for, the evidence of things not seen."

What we desire becomes evident by what we have faith for. What is it that you believe for and who is it that you believe in? Look past the surface, lukewarm, wishy-washy desire, the one that changes with every whim. Search deep within your heart, past the walls and booby traps. What holds your confidence? If you are uncertain as to where your faith lies, evaluate your life. What are the things you see? Don't like the view? What you see may be a result of what you believe. Not buying it? Try listening to what you say.

"[23] Keep thy heart with all diligence; for out of it are the issues of life."
Proverbs 4:23

"...for of the abundance of the heart his mouth speaketh."
Luke 6:45

The things that are in your heart show up in your life. And whatever is in your heart comes out of your mouth. Words don't have to be profane to curse. Words that confess the fear and doubt that you believe in your heart can curse your dreams. If you believe for the dim and grim and speak gloom over your life everyday, that is what you will see. To change what is in front of you would mean a change in what you believe and what you say.

God has promised all of his children a "happily ever after." The climax or turning point in your life is when you give your life to Christ. When you accept Him as Lord and savior, the rising conflict and crisis that were present become resolved. Psalms 23:1-5 provide the details to your story.

> "¹*The LORD is my shepherd; I shall not want.* ²*He maketh me to lie down in green pastures: he leadeth me beside the still waters.* ³*He restoreth my soul: he leadeth me in the paths of righteousness for his name's sake.* ⁴*Yea, though I walk through the valley of the shadow of death, I will fear no evil: for thou art with me; thy rod and thy staff they comfort me.* ⁵*Thou preparest a table before me in the presence of mine enemies: thou anointest my head with oil; my cup runneth over.*"
> Psalms 23:1-5

In God we have all that we need, He takes care of us. In Him we enjoy comfort and peace. Any broken place is healed and we are able to walk the path that is pleasing unto Him. The dragons you had to fight and slay in dark caverns were nothing to fear because God Almighty was with you. You will feast on His abundance no matter who opposes you. There is so much in store, that you can't hold it all. After all of this, after the battles He's won and new walk with Christ in heavenly pastures, we see the conclusion. We see the promise for the "happily ever after."

> "⁶*Surely goodness and mercy shall follow me all the days of my life: and I will dwell in the house of the LORD for ever.*"
> Psalms 23:6

The princess who rides off into the sunset is you. Her coach is followed by God's certain goodness and definitive mercy for her now, then, and eternity. Look at the punctuation. Once again, it is a period. There are no further thoughts, room for discussion, or means for debate. The ending is certain and so is your ever after.

It's up to you to choose the desired conclusion. Nothing you do can change the structure of the story. Only the details of how you get to the end can change. The rising conflict may rise for a longer period or a secondary may follow the primary, but noting you could ever do could change the outcome that God has planned for you.

> "²⁸ *And we know that in all things God works for the good of those who love him,*[j] *who*[k] *have been called according to his purpose.* ³¹*What, then, shall we say in response to this? If God is for us, who can be against us?* ³²*He who did not spare his own Son, but gave him up for us all—how will he not also, along with him, graciously give us all*

things? ^{38}For I am convinced that neither death nor life, neither angels nor demons,$^{[m]}$ neither the present nor the future, nor any powers, ^{39}neither height nor depth, nor anything else in all creation, will be able to separate us from the love of God that is in Christ Jesus our Lord."
Romans 8:28, 31-32, 38-39 NIV

Trust him. Believe him. What he says is the truth.

Take an up-close look at your life. Magnify all areas, especially those that are hidden from the naked eye. You may discover aspects of your being that you didn't know existed, or simply forgot were there.

A beautiful, vibrant, woman lies hidden beneath the surface. The rays of her light are blotted by a cold, hard, drab exterior formed in response to trying situations and unforeseeable circumstances. Or the bubbly, seemingly cheerful exterior may be an illusion, a facade for what really lingers in the shadows.

Hatred, lies, deceit, envy, and other organisms of sin are like viruses that seek to attack the righteous spirit that lives within. No matter how diminutive, the presence of sin alters true identity. If left unchecked, it can continue on its mission to kill every living word sewn into your heart.

The purpose of the devil is to deceive and alter your perspective of self, so that you won't live the life God has planned. With this knowledge in mind, take another evaluation of your identity. If the microscopic view of you doesn't resemble what God sees and says, change the lens, take another look. Each glimpse in the mirror shows a reflection of Him that lives and rules inside of you.

All women are created in the beautiful image of the Almighty God and are destined for greatness. If things don't look so great right now, keep living by faith. You know how the beginning commenced, have knowledge of the present. Through the word of God, you also have insight into the ending of your story. As the pages turn, the final chapter will conclude…

"And she lived Happily Ever After!"

About the Author

Tiffany L. Bride is a published writer, public speaker, motivator, wife and mother of two. She writes Moments of Motivation, providing daily encouragement to readers. Mrs. Bride is currently pursuing a M.A. in Marriage and Family Therapy as well as holds a M.B.A. in finance and a B.B.A in Risk Management. She strives to inspire those she encounters through her words, sentiments, and Christian living.

Made in the USA
Charleston, SC
24 September 2010